The 80th
Monologue

Zarra Hitsburg

Contents Page

The Preface

Chapter 1 The 80th Monologue

Chapter 2 Egos Over Peace

Egos Over Peace: The Poetry   50

Chapter 3 Dedicated to the Love Anthem

Chapter 4 Journey 08

Journey 08: The Poetry   164

Acknowledgements   200

The Preface

It's been over ten years of writing the 80th Monologue in which I began to consistently write at the age of nineteen. I never once stopped to think that my dialogue of poetic literature would transform into a book. I just wrote what I knew, what I saw and my thoughts. Mentally conceptualising economic and mass systems, human relations, socialisations, cognitive conditioning, and the overall world we live in was something I had always questioned from young and so paying attention to global systems was something I had always recognized. It was always easy for me to think outside of the box and more so outside of this paradigm of reality and the constructed systems of supreme…. I just found it easier to write about.

Having been a poetic writer before any other genre, my first love within creative writing was always to write about the social relations within love all of which scribbled from my fingers with ease. Writing linguistically came with ease to me from as early as primary school. Moving into secondary school I began to develop my writing skills into script writing with various plots and actors and often including my friends as characters within the play as per their request and handing out the papers around class for my school friends to read in hope that the teacher would not catch us whilst in lesson. And so, moving forward into my late teenage years it was at nineteen that I returned to writing poetic literature whilst mixing this with my previous curiosity for sociology, which is how the 80th Monologue was birthed.

The power of reading is tremendous, the places knowledge can take your mind is amazing once understood appropriately and used positively. However, with this in mention, this leads me on to simply debate that within the strategy of education, is all information not given to us via an author who also referenced information from another author who also read upon knowledge written via another author and so forth. To explain, the regurgitation of knowledge can be the construct of education, once needing another reference of someone else's comprehension of theory to then validate our own given information. Leaving one to question what makes information, literature, the linguistics of language and its full etymology of its transformation into understandings of fact, fiction, beliefs, and knowledge whilst captured between its philosophy of ethical moralities between wrong and right.... right?

And so, it can be argued that all information is just regurgitated knowledge via another person's perspective, unless this was evidence-based research then of course this would change the discourse of information gathered. However, if one must continue to reference another person's work to validate their own, then where is the authenticity within the philosophy of knowledge? Leaving one to question upon 'who standardizes' the epistemology of new and old ideologies?

When deciding to turn these writings into a book of poetic, spoken and creative literature, I wanted it to be a full embodiment of my own independent knowledge and not someone else's. Of course, one must read and study another person's information of knowledge in order to help heighten their own understandings, if not then how else would we educate ignorant or blinded minds and therefore the sharing of knowledge is subsequently a powerful transfer of information. This transfer mentioned, has helped to expand, and theorize my theory of written work. However, when deciding to publish the 80th Monologue into a book, I had much preferred to keep this book as authentic as I could, whilst still writing from a place of knowledge, theory, digested information, ideologies, and overall given wisdom that I understood whilst using the essence of one's experience to advocate this. Throughout this entire book I have synchronized both my poetic literature and my own independent theories as a collective combination to support the two comprehensions between understanding and knowledge.

Overall, this book is a conundrum of the depiction of critical thinking, poetry, independent theory, knowledge, and experience, all of which focuses upon the anthropology between society and the sub conscious being. The readings but more so the creative poetry in this book is a 'small' monologue of my own given understandings thus commencing from the age of nineteen to thirty as I intentionally stopped writing this book by the time that I arrived at thirty.

I am aware that some individuals may believe that I may have read the Bible in order to write this book or that I have been reading sociological books from an early age. However, I never grew up in a church and I never studied the Bible or the Quran or any biblical book to initiate this book and nor did I read around sociology to begin writing this book, this book commenced years before my hands reached for sociological understandings, with my readings upon sociological theory commencing a few years later.

Chapter 1
The 80th Monologue

"We must remove ourselves from our own disposition of self if we wish to educate ourselves" (Z,Hitsburg)

Introduction

When we strip back the systems of oppression, conformity, formation and conduct, the revolution of social media and the strain to acquire luxury goods; only then will we begin to strip back the continuous entity used to control and regulate the world: fear. Once you recognise and critically understand the depths of fear and how it has been used to keep people in the constant mental struggle of financial instability, you then begin to see how much global systems can sabotage the unconscious and sub-conscious mind away from one's true priorities, moral integrity, and happiness. All of which overall keeps all individuals' attentions away from being there authentic and conscious self. It leaves it open to question the level of justice, empathy, and morality within civilisation in today's current existence.

My theory behind the 80th Monologue attempts to acutely breakdown the societal systems and the images we see every day thus including propaganda, socialisation, poverty, conformity, capitalism, democracy, hypocrisy, and western industrialization causing a loss of consciousness of self. Therefore, the chapter the 80th Monologue investigates in greater detail upon how governmental systems, functions and socialisms has governed and systematically constructed employment and sabotages individuals true state of mental consciousness, whilst highlighting how the entity of 'fear' of financial instability has been used as tool to control civilisation causing mass zombies.

The 80th Monologue as a chapter explores how people within society at large have been taught to conform to structural rules however, not taught to positively, critically or consciously critique new information, status quo, tradition, systems, and rules. The 80th Monologue continues to attempt to briefly breakdown how a capitalist society keeps the functioning of systematic poverty and wealth present, in a western world which seeks for equality but lives by capitalistic laws. This chapter also goes on to explain the dynamics between hierarchy and equality and the sub-conscious sabotaged mind. Lastly this chapter gives light into the brief ethics of a free world and how change for the greater good within humanity begins with the individual called 'self'.

E very day we leave our houses and begin a new day may it be going to work, liaising with others, going to school, doing the grocery shopping, and attending events or parties or other various means of socialisation. Socialising with others in any scale is a way of life and we do It every day 'effortlessly'.

With so many laws, policies, legislations, and systems of conduct it can also be seen that those in positions of power and influence, and the information from history have altered the way in which people interact with others due to its ideological frame works of systematic normality of which has all been strategized not to cause a threat to the status quo within supremacy. Thus, impacting upon the way people perceive each other and even how people view themselves.

To explain, we are governed by a multitude of laws, acts and legislations put in place to positively help give a voice to the minority, fight against deprivation, and give rights to all those within humanity thus for an overall equal society. However, these are the same systematic laws, acts and legislations which can adversely work against a person and can marginalize and oppress a person or groups, just disguised with a notion of 'equality for all'. This oxymoron can be dangerous when attempting to live in a world which organises equality but is governed by capitalistic stratifications. Often leaves one to question how this pretence of equality and capitalism works successfully in conjunction with each other when ultimately a westernised capitalistic world enabled one person in charge of democracy within a dis-position of hierarchy and power to say differently.

Societal Consciousness Vs Authentic Consciousness

A minority or arguably a great deal of individuals in today's contemporary times are very much induced by social media, reality tv shows, acquiring financial wealth, engrossed in superficial looks and/or appearing to be a person of importance via the validation of social media platforms. Validated by how many followers or likes a person has of which, all attributes towards increasing a shallow minded society of who is more interested with things that doesn't merit them as a person, help others or add depth to their day in general. Through critical observation I recognised the endless injustices that people wake up to everyday whilst being aware of the conscious sabotage that the world can enter us into. People's level of consciousness has been in distraction due to the superficiality's mentioned above in which makes it much harder to create meaningful relations with others within society. Due to this It can be critiqued that people have possibly become de-sanitized to the injustices that we view everyday via i.e., via our television screens and smart phones, thus changing the emotionalism of individuals and society at large, all of which can impact upon individuals' level of care and feelings towards/for others. Therefore, it can be questioned that due to the increased access of smart phones and social media that multiple agencies of information may have normalised the terror people have become accustomed to (as appose to just a few technologies such as the television and radios in previous centuries). Therefore, does this adversely also indicate that the people within the 21st society are now much less empathetic for the care for others than in comparison to previous generations? This within itself could also be changing the emotionalisms of society at large and peoples need for gratification as appose to patience.

The national and global systematic systems of conditioning can leave some feeling stifled once they utterly understand and see the systems

4

of the world for what it really is in its most transparent form.

How can we expect a person to be there true joyful and happy self when bogged down with bills, debt or other financial pressures that must be paid each month? Most would say money is not important however, how much does this line still exist when 'free' money presents itself. We live in a world of systems and institutions which dictate and expect conformity. From an early age we are taught to conform, and this is apparent in the schooling and educational systems, to which this very system can educate a person to be an upheld employable citizen when in the working world. Everything for people in society has been systematically constructed to us from an early age, which is another reason why people grow up sticking to what they know because it feels safe or some become a product of their environment because to think outside the box, to ask too many questions or being too opinionated becomes troublesome, menacing and overall threatens a senior persons disposition of hierarchy, influence, power and status quo within governmental institutions, employment, organisations, education, domestically, family household and so forth. Therefore, people who go against power such as this pose an un-conventional threat structurally, economically, and globally. And, in a world where individuals are categorised and therefore pre dispositioned into a box of which dictates how they are seen and when they can speak; threating status quo was always a tough position to embody when attempting to dismantle the frameworks that built oppression, hierarchy and systems and much more. Because the sacrifice to dismantle this framework needs great courage to critique the rotation of integration. This is because the person may be at risk of their reputation being under scrutiny from those who do seek to understand, are ignorant or expect conformity.

Sub-Conscious Systematic Socialisation Vs Conscious Social Integration

If we were to attempt to de construct hierarchy but more so the rotation of socialisation and attempt to breakdown the frameworks of a constructed socialized society then we must start by looking at socialisations beginning, middle and its 'end' and you may see how its circular functioning can shape society's social integration. To explain, circulating socialisms is done through altering the individual's conscious and sub conscious thought process of the individual mind. Therefore, infiltrating what a person considers to be normal, acceptable, threating, and positive etc all of which can create preconceived views, prejudice, stereotyping, judgment and many more.

This is governed through standardized and systemized perpetuated imagery of the media's representations of given information regarding knowledge, race, gender, sexuality, colourism, disability, ethnicities, religion and so forth. All to which shapes individuals' identities and grouped identities due to how people are portrayed in the media, resulting in the mind to become conditioned to see and view things, acts and people through the ideological constructions of normality. Thus, increasing stereotyping, prejudice, marginalization, and oppression plus much more to which it is apparent here that systematic conditioning formulates in the mind first before anywhere else if wanting to dominate or destruct an individual or groups of people. In addition to this, systematic representations of normality can continue to alter societies state of morality and it is these very systems of supremacy which dictate what people should view as right and wrong. This leads to the shaping of how people see themselves in comparison to others, which can lead to or cause competition amongst people and this overall another example of how capitalism continues to manifest in western societies.

Overall, all the above has an impact upon how people determined their own perception regarding what is reality, how they conscious and sub consciously process information, how they view people and things or those of who are different to them but also impacting upon a person's views and understandings. To which conclusively may generate discrimination and division amongst people thus due to the fear of the unknown. If fear within social relations is present within society, then this may create a culture of 'normality'. Leading to some people to stick to what the person or community knows in fear of social integration, because it feels safer to not interrupt the routine or functioning's within societal or social integration. However, a person who fails to socialise with those who are different to them is not just governed through fear but could also be due to a superior mindset thus believing they and their people (a person's heritage, race or area that they live in) may be better than others or are not like other people etc. We are all in the circuit of systematic civilisation of which can dictate how this formulates when people integrate and socialise with each other.

However, disrupting the normality of systems within socialisation socially and globally would mean disrupting society's traditional norms of functioning. All of which comes with the sacrifice to a person's reputation of which may include a person being at risk of being seen as a person of whom is disruptive, exaggerated, problematic and an outcast etc when attempting to question the systems of oppression and much more. So much so that if a person is depicted with the usage of the above labels (i.e. in the media, socially etc) in actuality it only adversely re- enforces stereotyping, ignorance, biasedness, patriarchy, sexism, racism, culturalism, and marginalization when journalist over exaggerate the truth. However, these are the same mass systems or propaganda, television, entertainment and music industries, and social media which need those of whom attain the bare faced courage to disturb the peace to speak out loud in order to reform and transform what it means to socialize with others authentically and with little judgment, with a hope of forming a new kind of socialisation with newly created fundamentals built on the moralities of love, equality, honesty, respect, humility, and justice.

It clear that when people uneducated themselves to re-educate themselves and adopt a teamwork ethic and it new attitudes of thinking are consolidated, this may lead to the discourse of societal socialisation to enter a new period of change. People must improve the way they live with each other by building a better understanding with how they see each other and give others the benefit of the doubt before concluding, thus done by listening, giving empathy, giving respect, giving positive affirmations, giving support, accept faults, content with being wrong, eliminate hierarchy in all forms, communicate, be honest more, be accountable for their actions more and of course love more.

Hierarchy Vs Equality

Power is shaped by hierarchy and all concepts of power are grouped on identity. The linage within historical and social systems is which dictates to a certain level how people in the 21st society engage with each other, of which this can be argued that it may be possibly based on how the dynamic of power within various groups identities are categorised and if categorisation amongst people is present then an unequal disposition of hierarchy over others is also present thus causing a duality of conflict. For example, rich and poor and young and old this duality of conflict can also seep into race, disability, ethnicities and much more) and so forth all of which results in a spectrum between higher and lower to be present as overall one person or group has been categorised in front or before another therefore causing there to be a clear distinction of inequality.

And so, what we are concisely examining here is the dynamics between hierarchy, power, and identity, thus shaped by ideologies of mis-informed education, ignorance and or fear. Leading people within the world to be fearful of one another thus causing great suffering, poverty, wealth, and division.

When we look at civilisations integration between each other in the physical form and western societies strive for equality within a capitalistic functioning, it can lead one to also question what is the metaphysical understanding or even meaning of categorisations, systems, hierarchy, and power? Somethings maybe beyond us and it is only the actual individual who can create their own foundations and discover their own purpose upon what and who mean more to them. As a result, all people can do is always attempt to keep things simple and leave worldly practices such as pride, jealousy, revenge, and anger behind them and move forward to openness, honesty, growth, support and helping one another in order to create a new system of what I call a love ethic thus recreating equality, prosperity, teamwork, and peace for all persons both local, nationally, and globally.

Therefore, if love (within any ethic) is possibly the nucleus of which shapes unity then the pro found differences we have been categorised within people's identity of differences can be seen in a positive manner. Seeing differences with a positive outlook may lead society on a whole to become stronger and no longer fearful of others when differences are present. Because, once higher systems, constructs, ideologies, categorisations, labelled identities are dismantled and detached from a person's cognitive though process, this could possibly alter a person's metaphysical and/or sub/conscious understanding leading people to give 'possibly' those of whom are different to them the benefit of doubt and to see the beauty to the differences in front of them. Overall helping positive integrations to take place between grouped identities of who share a common denominator of 'acceptance' between them and others.

Self VS SELF

The transformation of self can take place in any way a person sees fit for purpose however, the power of reading is a great phenomenon. When receiving any form of knowledge, one must read intentionally with an open attitude and place themselves as a reader or person who seeks to understand and is confidently okay with being a beginner when receiving new information. However, when putting this into practice the person of whom is receiving the new information must not receive this information form a place of feeling victimised, with arrogance of knowing everything, personalise the information, negatively challenge the opposition, or be emotionally attached to the content of information being received/communicated when in conversation. If any of these barriers are present then the conversation is not one of reciprocation and far from transformative as the information is instead being received by the other person through feelings of belittlement, insecurity, or ignorance.

To remove yourself from your own feelings and the disposition of 'self' will enable people to truly educate themselves, learn from others and grow a person's minds. So much so that when one hears truth speak, they shan't feel triggered by their own experiences and or faults by what has been shared, because the person would have found a deep acceptance within their own past actions and trauma. Enabling them to listen to others when receiving new information and when part taking in conversations with others. When acceptance of self, others and inner love is present, it can help to enable one to heal from inner turmoil and progress them towards growth. Therefore, the intake of new information should not disrupt or annoy the person of whom disagrees because the core of their own self-acceptance would actualise them to accept that each person sees everything differently. To continue, the ability to accept differences and knowing that each person knows different things will physically illustrate its self when a person enters into conversations or when receiving new information or direction from others as the conversation will be fluid with both persons able to listen and learn from each other without taking things personal but more so okay to hear things from a different perspective, with a personal objective to broaden their own knowledge and therefore happy to part take in conversations with people of who share understanding at various levels of knowledge. So much so that one won't be so easily offended when receiving criticism because their self-acceptance should lead them to simply accept the situation/conversation at hand. Of course, one must stress that the above descriptions all depend on who the person (of who is receiving criticism) is speaking and listening to and more importantly if they respect the person of whom they are conversating with. However, with all the above explained; if a person is yet to remove themselves from themselves (to gain a broader understanding) then the reciprocation of sharing knowledge and entering into dialogue with people who yet to accept themselves may come at a high cost possibly not worth paying.

Greater Good

If people globally do not take on a new perception of thinking starting within themselves first, and accepting their actions, decisions, positives, faults, and the full diaspora of self, then how can we expect this transformation to become a positive synergy of growth in order to merge with others? As making change for self primarily, should be done for the greater good within ourselves firstly, secondly for others, our communities and society at large. If this morality is not accepted within us first, then consumerism, shallowness, superiority, controlled systems and constructs, fear, mental health, inequality, poverty, ignorance, marginalisation's, abuse, crime, racism, cultural ignorance, judgements, and preconceived perceptions and much more will continue to dictate the world we live in. Raw agriculture, environments and all forms of nature are in its own time zone and will not wait for anyone and evolution in any aspect will continue to manifest regardless of if it is good or evil. Therefore, fight the good fight and let love win.

The 80th Monologue the poetic literature explores the regulation of civilisation and systematic oppression within society and continues to highlight the discrepancies of inequalities within global systems. This chapter has been written for new readers and the readers who enjoy critical thinking, and for those of who enjoy socialisation in its authentic form. And lastly this chapter has been written for those of who enjoy sitting back and being self-centred in a world with so many distractions.

The 80th Monologue
The Poetry

Metaphysical Mind

Take my head
And put it on your shoulders
I don't want to think tonight
And now my borrowed mind is now yours
And you can begin to think like me
Hopefully, you'll see what I see
Maybe then you'll start to understand what I mean
Welcome to the 80th Monologue the poetry

A -Z

All aboard

First stop London

Second stop

...Global

Travelling World

Our difference of image creates segregation
Our level of wealth creates a competition of winners and losers
Our gender creates expectations that differ from males to females
But these creations serve for what purpose if we are all living in a
travelling world

Systematic Poverty

*Unless all individuals and those in the position of influence use the
power of love for all of humanity in order to care for the empathy of all
existence;*
If this is not shared equally
*Then we will continue to be new revolutionised slaves of employment
Against the systematic struggle of poverty*

Criticality

Your own perception of reality is critically moulded by the structure and virtue of society
But true freedom lies in the ability to critically understand your own humanisation
In acceptance of yourself and others in praxis with life
Which is reciprocated through the act of love and courage

Fear

We fight and kill each other
Because of fear, anger, poverty, power, systems, greed,
and other means
Due to the fear of the unknown
Due to the fear of opposition
Due to the fear of being out of control
When all we really need is to......
Love, help, give, and receive and with this
We'd be one step closer to peace

Platform 80

We are all living a contemporary life with the modern struggle of
wealth

Buzz...Buzz...Buzz

There goes your routine alarm clock

Wages woke you up

Walking in crowds

Walking through crowds

The scent of individual aromas clouding the atmosphere

With one breathe to another

Face to face with each other

Holding on to the handlebars

So that we don't fall into one another

.... guess we all must reach our destination, involuntary with each other

The hustle and bustle

The businessman with his suit and tie

The sleepy passengers

Those who apply there make up passengers

The run

The chase

The division

The diversity

All in one space

In between London's yellow and red lines

Walking to work to earn money

But walking through poverty to get there

My journey towards a place where I pay taxes

Leads me to walk pass the

The homelessness

The wealthy

The drug users who remain keen

And those trying to make a living through things

Work: the socioeconomic system of employment or lack of employment

The TFL pragmatic operations of winners and losers that I see every day

on a journey we are all constructed to make

Social Media

We are in a revolutionary
As social media continues to revolutionize how one communicates to another
Merging a deception upon communication and integration
Causing a binary upon reality and deception
Misleading others upon the conceptualisation of how we live with each other
Social media created a conundrum of disposable relations
Therefore, dialogue is everything
Recognise those who talk to you
Within society's current socio-economic climate
We are all examples of victimised financial oppression
With the weight of whatever struggle is real to you
And only positivity and faith will keep you
Only real ones will talk with you
Only self-reflection can answer you
Only teamwork can progress you
Keep going
You'll get there soon

Simon Says

Legislations, policies, laws, and procedures were put in place within
society for equality in the workplace and beyond
To protect a person's welfare
To conduct a civilised society and overall
For the justice of human rights
Because ultimately....
Hierarchy and authority creates conflict
So, we attempt to strive for equality
In a world built upon industrialisation which birthed capitalism
This is hypocrisy!
This was the biggest missed conception put in place to fool you
When the oxymoron within the parallels between equality and
capitalism is unachievable
As ultimately justice may never be achieved within this circuit
As these legislations are the same acts that 'protect' us but
simultaneously marginalise us
Democracy is far and few in between
Voting gave you a dream
Equality could never be achieved
Because ultimately capitalism enabled one person or one institution
with the power to say differently

Globalized You

We are all victims of a globalised world

With the pressure of societal norms to fit into an identity that is not the description of you

But just a boxed paradigm of how society attempts to shape who you are

Globalised You Part II

Where are you?

What is your name?

Are you sane?

Are you okay?

Tell me all about you

Not the things that you believe make you, you

But how you see yourself above the names and labels

Or did you enable systems to shape you............

I hope not

I call it: living on the surface of life

That's fine

As everyone's different right?

But allow me to exhale this creative literature to you

People all over the world are everyday living in a social construct

Governed by systematic oppressions

With the entity of fear used to financially oppress you

Therefore, shaping the virtues of the sub-conscious being

This leads to some becoming conditioned into a system without the ability to critique obstructions

Then you become socially abducted

Be your own social construct

When your social self can be segregated from the frameworks that created this fake culture of reality and the real you is shown above the systematic and social normatives

And if troubled, conditioned, or systematically controlled minds continue to judge you

They're just perpetuating the political bullshit that made it

Therefore, they aren't sh**

They have no armour
They are what others say they are
However, you can be your own conductor
You can be bold or subserviently self-centred and confident within
yourself and mind
Because now, your character cannot be defined

New Generation

Ultimately, we want to teach our children to have love, respect, equality, gratitude, humility, honour, kindness, honesty, self- reflection, accountability, acceptance, teamwork, principles, values, morals, and goals

All of which can and will help oneself and the care for others
So that we raise a generation of critical thinkers and unity in the new age society
Imagine the possibilities of change

Scholar

Learn about what you don't know
To challenge something, you now know
Learn another person's craft
But create your own blueprint
One must watch those who conquered great things before them
So that you can re emulate your own success to a higher level
Be a scholar
Listen
Observe
Then act
All people who are considered great were gifted with a talent
Listen and learn upon how others used there's
Then illustrate the perfection of yours

Language

The most effective way to learn is to listen
The most effective way to learn is through communication
The power of words within conversations speaks volumes
Language speaks communication
Language speaks time
Language speaks empathy
Language speaks unity
Language speaks listening
Language speaks a million things
Language speaks we care

The Power of Divide and Concur

In order to do this, you must

1. *Make them hate themselves*

And most importantly

2. *Make them unaware of their own destruction*

And with this you will have a group of people who oppress one another

Due to the differences that does not define them

You'll be the best replicate of white supremacy which has conditioned you into a salve mentality

If you self-reciprocate your own dislike, preferences or hate for your own people

So, the next time you view the black woman as ugly or the black man as worthless

Continue to fight and kill one another

Or divide each other through your own preferences of light skin or dark skin

You'll continue to sustain insecurities within your own race

The oppression and value of skin complexion within colourism is one of the most powerful divisions ever created

Once you associate the various complexions of brown skin

Under the categories of oppression within class, gender, beauty, wealth and so forth

Leading these same categorisations to re-emulate and sustain 'Black oppression'

Impacting the black people financially, romantically and sociably

In due course

Altering the black race upon how they integrate but more so how they view each other

With some judging other black people for the same skin that they also
wear
Ultimately leading black people to suffer from self- internalised racism

Colourism is the sibling to racism
The dynamic may have changed
But a colourist and a racist mind bare no difference
Their eyes look through the same lens just with different frames

Skin complexions association within either upper and lower class,
beautiful or ugly, aggressive or non-aggressive; has been created by
one man's ideological objectification of hierarchy upon brown skin
I.e., The slave division: In the house maid or out in the garden doing
field work
Your still black......you're still a slave
When ultimately black remains black in a world ran by whites

If you act upon these discrepancies
Then you're a product of the racist white man's mentality
'The puppet'
Who's strengthening power into white supremacy
And continuing to keep slavery alive
Through the enslavement of your own mind

The 80th O'clock News

I turned on the TV and saw destruction and death in Palestine and the
news reporter spoke about those killed as if it was 'another report'
I turned on the TV and saw parents broken because all three of their
children died in a plane crash and the media's tone reported this storey
as it was 'just another report'
I flicked through the channels and heard of a few people reported
missing whilst on a flight and the news's images, tone, editing, and
information reported this as a 'shocking storey'
Pause…. let's take a deeper analysation into the information being
conveyed to us

We're seeing death, pain, war, and loss on our televisions
Never forget the power and sorrow of these images
As what you are seeing on your television screen is repeated every day
until it becomes normal for you to view this type of destruction
Repetitive news and images such as these sub consciously can enable
us to become de sensitized to the pain, we are seeing others experience
However, do not let this lack of empathy become a normalised message
within your own reality
In addition, do not let conspiracy become your reality
The real reality is that people are struggling, people are dying
And it is compassion for others which is missing

Channel TV

The TV is powerful tool
And the luxury of owning a television is no longer an item of luxury
But an expectant item within every 21st century household
Advocating its messages into each person's personal home
With just a click of a button
Don't conceptualise the medias reports as just another news report
Those dead and missing is not a report
Your witnessing sorrow and sadness
Keep empathy near to you
Marxist theory of the media reveals the ultimate power of conditioning
individuals mentally is by
synonymously shaping society's cultural and social norms through
repetitive images of ideologies and actions via revolutionary tools
Tools such as your television screens, smart phones, propaganda. social
media and magazines
But don't become a replica of this
Critique this
Create your own reality and
Structure your own normality

365

You should refuse to be an example of institutionalise oppression
Even when you are faced with categorised degradation
Tell them that you shan't be a part of this generalised population
Be the individual that doesn't fit into the stratification of financial
income for the exchange of your identity through employment
Due to the new age slavery that employed it

Distortions of Mediated Fact or Fiction

*People get personally and politically annoyed when blacks and ethnic
minorities are represented in the media in a negative form
However, do recognise that stereotyped representations of people
come from the truth
However, those in power both overtly, passively, and negatively
exaggerate the truth
The injustice of these exaggerated truths consciously and
subconsciously impacts people upon how we view each other, perceive
each other, how we approach others and overall, how we socialise with
each other
Conclusively shaping how we socialise with each other socially,
professionally, and globally
However, let us explore this*

*One must analyse, accept, and evaluate fact from fiction
In actual fact these representations represent the true inequalities of
society
Because an oppressed group or an oppressed community of people do
not hold the power to represent themselves in a positive image via
propaganda
As those in power hold control upon how each group or person is
represented
Therefore, leaving the truth to become a quiet whisper upon
exaggerated representations
Subconsciously impacting the way, we view each other
By the normalized distortions of images between
Fact and fiction
Deception and Reality*

Stereotypes and Perception

Oppression and Power

Truth and False

Injustice and Justice

Racism and Equality

And ultimately

Good and Bad

Leaving society at large to become fearful of one another

Fear: such a powerful entity needed in order to continue to sustain divisions between people

Such a needed emotion in order to keep standardized images, poor fictions, and poor ideologies present

Enabling fear to be a transformative weapon

A double edge sord

Of which when used by those of whom choose 'power' over influence

Enables conductors to cognitively, overtly, and most importantly to synonymously reinforce and sustain the empowerment of white superiority

Normalising uneducated blindness

Normalising systematic oppression

Normalising the oppression of an oppressed group

Of whom is still gasping for the freedom to be seen

Subsequently enabling the rich to remain rich and the poor to remain poor

Whites to be seen as good and/or racist

And blacks to be seen as aggressive or hostile

And so forth

When ultimately our differences are what make the world amazing

There's beauty to our differences

And difference can birth teamwork

But only when love, equality and justice is present

Therefore, it is not so much the negative representations that need to change
It is the inequalities of the world that need to change
It is the conductors of systemic oppression and institutional racism that needs to change
Therefore, overall: It is the people in the world that needs to change

Let us applaud the brave
Those who are willing to risk their position of comfortability for the sake and care of others
So that the oppressed can be seen but also heard
In order to breakdown racial constructs, prejudice, micro aggressions, stereotyping, inequality's, injustice, and exaggerated ideologies
Resulting in eyes to no longer to be blind
Uneducated minds to seek for more time to read
Resulting in individuals to see the person before pre perceptions
Birthing............. Global peace
Middle fingers to those who choose conflict over love
Ignorance over understanding
Pride over reason
They may never understand the peace that humility brings

However, peace never came easy
As peace needs the vocality of reflection, honesty, accountability, and acceptance in order to create equality
For the greater good
Given to her, him, she, he, and you

If peace is needed, then growth is the enabler
Therefore, society needs growth
Growth takes time
But first growth needs to be recognized
Recognize that the attributes of outspokenness, love and courage is
what needs to be transparent
Thus, creating the emancipation of a movement of which needs to be
fiercely acted upon
But also spoken 'with'
As communication is powerful
And language enables education
And its education that can inhibit change
And it starts with a simple letter 'I'

Care

When a warm heart turns cold
It will eventually become dishearten
Abracadabra!
The heart disappears
And the element of care
Will no longer be there

Commodities

When you become a commodity to the money you earn

You will realise what and who means more to you

Chapter 2

Egos Over Peace

"Embody a positive self-fulfilling prophecy within oneself as you have nothing to prove" (Z, Hitsburg)

Introduction

C onfidence: It is to be admired. Those of whom walk with no care in the world for what others think about them is to be considered notably attractive. However, when it is confidence that later becomes cockiness, brags about what they have or those of who think that they are better than others Is not an energy most would like to endorse or possibly be around.

We are all at points guilty of being vain or being victim to consumerism as we cannot always run away from the pressures that society and peer pressure place upon us and there is nothing wrong with wanting the finer things in life and looking after our material assets as people generally work hard for them, and so they are there to be enjoyed. However, it only becomes worrying when these luxury goods become of extreme importance, with some people feeling empty when losing material goods therefore unknowingly these items become a definition upon how some feel about themselves, how they want others to see them, and what moves their happiness. This is when a selfish culture creates the phrase of 'dog eat dog' world becomes apparent as the selfishness within this mantra creates room for greed thus leading to the domination of self over the compassion for others.

My theory behind Egos Over Peace attempts beaks down the ideologies of constructed socialisms and class categorisations within a capitalist society due to the vanity within consumerism and how this may create a superficial mindset for people within society at large, thus shaping how people see themselves, how they see others and how people can become a part of a conforming culture when attempting to keep up appearances. Therefore, this chapter explores in depth upon how vanity and material acquisition amplifies global consumerism, hierarchy, judgments, and poor perceptions, whilst highlighting how this at the same time breaks down unity, trust, opportunities, social mixing, and equality within social groups in society at large due to class categorisations plus more.

Lastly Egos over Peace discusses how westernized constructs can shape individuals' values but it also continuing to explain how financial gain sabotages one's personal growth and lack of true inner confidence. One must intensely stress that the content written in this chapter 'does not apply to all people' and it will always be a matter of theory for some but truth for others. One must continue to stress that the ideologies behind Egoes Over Peace as a chapter will not and does not apply to all persons, nor is any one immune from the understandings within this chapter as were 'all' victims to the influences we are exposed to. Perfection was never perfect.

I n a visually enticed society, most people fall victim to the assimilation of societal values due to superficiality and external acceptance to be seen well, therefore overall losing a sense of self.

It clear that sex sells which is a narrative which works well in society's product of appeal to which this is also used when conducting and controlling people/society at large, thus resulting in successful consumerism and mass production; all of which gives the sense of stability to both the individual and society when financial wealth is gained. However, the accumulation of wealth is not always shared to others who may be struggling with poverty and so forth. A shallow mind would believe that there looks or how they carry themselves is sufficient to what they consider important to them (some say this is not the case but subconsciously it is for some). This superficiality can include how one is dresses, the cost of clothes that they buy and the expensive goods that they strive for all of which illustrate their level of financial wealth i.e., clothes, cars, jewellery and so forth. When vanity becomes such an apparent factor of importance for some individuals then it can easily create a character who becomes self-absorbed and more concerned with their appearance, the things that they own and more concerned with how they come across and the things that they buy, but where is this positioned when placed next to care and love for others? But do the things we buy really matter? Will one not feel externally full but internally empty? As human beings regardless of race, ethnicity, gender, sexuality, disability etc all person has an inner self and the more one consumes materials things or gravitates towards sexual attention is the more one's inner self becomes vacant and sabotaged but full of external clothing's and material possessions of which subsequently still leaves the inner self empty.

Vanity Vs Consumerism

Fashion itself which is a part of the objectification of beauty can be considered another tool used to dominate and conquer. It can be used as tool to construct power over others through its domination within its invisibility to move a person's mood and happiness thus causing a person to be intrigued and somewhat feeling valued to be noticed/seen as a person of whom 'looks good'.

I am sure we have all encountered characters of people of whom share the same unknowing values to what I have stated above. One must see the big picture with how society can easily shape a person's values and how they are seen by the things that a person's buys. There has been various contemporary artists, authors, journalists, humanitarians, historians, philosophers, and sociologists of whom have all discussed or aligned the depiction of art in praxis with fashion and spirituality. Subsequently most sociologist and philosophers etc conclude their findings towards the identical notion that the aesthetics of beauty within fashion can leave a person's inner self feeling unclothed.

If spiritual emptiness is present then one can only contend that people's lack of inner substance causes a lack of conscious and subconsciousness awareness, resulting in a lack of self-actualisation, let alone a lack of understanding, or accepting who they really are. Nevertheless, leading some people to continue a cycle of parental sins and more so to become a product of their environment and societies superficial values.

Societal influences and consumerism and the pressure to acquire can easily create an individual to become narcissistic, arrogant, vain, and selfish all of which is synonymously reared by social media, magazines, propaganda, competition, insecurities, and the daily imagery of perfection that people see every day due to mass media of consumption

44

and the lack of democracy of shared equality above materialism. If a selfish culture prevails then the increase of superficiality within society becomes even more prevalent. Superficiality is pivotal within the regulations of consumerism and imagery within our society. It can be easily contended that vanity heightens or creates greed and selfishness within a person, not only causing an inner emptiness but also leading to the individual's inner growth and ethics to love others to become of somewhat secondary importance. If self-love is vacant then the ability to love others will also become vacant because one must love themselves firstly to truly know how to love somebody else. And a world without love may leave people without the hunger to unite with others in a realm beyond the fashioned eye.

This leads me on to explain that the abduction of self-growth and self-actualization can enable a shallow minds lack of understanding (ignorance in simpler terminology) to negatively judge how they view others and what they think of others and, more importantly impacting upon how they approach others overall dictating the social groups that a person keeps themselves around. I am sure we have all heard people say things such as "he/she looks like a nice person". How many times have you heard statement such as this ? with the person of whom they were referring to being a person who was visually attractive? But what does a person have to look like to be considered 'a nice person'? what thresholds of normality must a person obtain to be considered 'nice' and what references or resources are people using to measure 'nice' under? What does nice actually look like? Does nice not look like everyone?

Perceptions & Judgement Vs Inclusion

To examine, a self-absorbed society can easily create unfair judgments, causing various inequalities within socialisms. This mindset of judgement can also filter through into employment therefore causing discrimination and impacting upon the opportunities or lack of opportunities for some ethnic minorities and not others. Overall leading to the disparities between rich and poor. All because a person may be different and does not visually fit the categories of what is considered normal or less threatening within employment or 'attractive' in romantic courting.

This leads me on to explain that these disparities of categorisations and social labelling's only help to increase and attain global and social divisions therefore creating inequalities and a lack of confidence for those people who do not 'fit in'. And these inequalities can easily filter into categories of race, gender, masculinity, femininity, beauty, wealthy, poverty and so forth.

Those of whom believe they are better than another (this is also sometimes done unknowingly as society can impact the subconscious state of mind and values as stated above) will cause some people to withhold from mixing with others of whom are different to them. All of which can be a contributing factor as to why divisions within societal categories such as 'class' are present and why the divisions between rich and poor are also still present. As there is no sharing of wealth, mixing of minds and creating friendships with those who are outlandishly different.

Overall, it is factors explained above as to why and how a shallow mind keeps the categories of oppression such race, class, gender, disability, sexuality, beauty (plus much more) and its inequalities and injustices present in everyday socialisms.

Due to all the above mentioned, most people primarily take people for face value thus causing others to be either weary of each other, in competition with others, jealous, envious, narcissistic, self-absorbed, causing some people to be strive to fashion fit in with their peers.

As the element of trust becomes sabotaged within society due to the rehearing of subconscious superficiality and conditioning (and other factors). People do not trust one another and anything of which looks different may poses as a threat to a person of who is also already fearful. When a lack of trust and acceptance is present then people naturally begin to guard themselves and some people deliberately present themselves in a way in which will be considered normal, acceptable, wealthy, beautiful, handsome, and so forth in order to be seen as acceptable and to fit in with others. However, their true inner confidence is still questionable because the strive to 'fit in' or to be seen as attractive or beautiful due to the assets or clothes a person's buys will not ever compensate for how they truly feel about themselves on the inside. However, this is subjective because how and why people present themselves to other people differs from person to person and some people can find a positive balance between superficiality and their inner self and so one must continue to keep an open mind regardless of how one dresses and how a person presents themselves.

If superficiality, pretentiousness, judgements, consumerism, wealth, stereotyping, racism, internalised racism, colonial mindsets, and lack of honesty becomes the root of society then the cohesion of trust, kindness and solidarity within humanity becomes a mere wind lost with a simple sight. As mentioned before, people with superficiality and societal values can easily become a pawn to society, enabling society to shape who they are, how they are seen, there true priorities, and values thus governed by the things that they buy. It is victims such as these who are intensely concerned with their appearance all of the time of who stay in a constant chase of financial wealth, with their happiness being governed by societal values due to the wealth they acquire. In summary a loss of identity within a person's inner self can become lost or owned due to and by the regulation of societies values.

As a result, the superficial world we now live in disables the element of kindness and trust to be shared from one person to another with ease due to preconceived perceptions and judgments upon others of who do not attain the same level of wealth, standardized attractive looks, or who are outlandishly different can and will jeopardises the element of peace within humanisations, socialisms, and communication due to the judgments upon others.

Inner Confidence Vs Societal Confidence

No one likes a show-off however most enjoy confidence of which is positively owned, the balance is to be fond of. Striving for the best, attempting to own assets, looking nice, having a great time and presenting ourselves to a certain standard was never a problem, though it becomes questionable when one's happiness is only confident when fully clothed in their best gear, attending only the finest events, and withdrawing/feeling uncomfortable when socialising with others who are different to themselves.

We can all admire a person's confidence but we all can respect confidence when it does not put down others or believe themselves to be better than others and gloat upon what they own. In conclusion, societal values and conditioned minds, over saturated images of beauty and fashion are all attributing factors to keeping the inequalities of injustice alive, thus taking away the great co-cohesion of integration between all people within civilisation.

Egos Over Peace the poetic literature has been written from a feministic perspective, a splurge of words which illustrate an authentic confidence within a female disposition in a patriarchal society, whilst show casing the inequalities between the battle of the sexes. Overall, Egoes Over Peace the poetry captures the balance of owned arrogance and authentic confidence and its resistance from societal expectations, sexism, judgments, conformity, and boundaries and enjoying the here and now.

Egos Over Peace
The Poetry

Egos Over Peace

Egos over peace
My imagination part two
The trade of morals for commodities
The trade of love for money
I feel different
I no longer believe
It's crazy how much you can stop believing in something
When you come out of a particular mind state
Now I only want what I can see
A visionary of wealth and nice things
Plus, other sins
Selfish actions
My arrogance disturbing the peace
My arrogance sheltering me
Doing things, I would never do if it were 2015
It scares me how quick time is flying
Feels like only the other day that it was seven years ago
When I wrote the 80th Monologue
And I held on to my faith and dreams
Guess I was asking for too much
Guess now I'm only thinking about me
I lust now I don't dream
I want now I don't need
Guess love made a monster out of me

$X = Y$

A male must know themselves as a man first

In order to enable them to understand a female

And the value of a woman

One can only be forced to snare in the face of those of who fail to learn

Fail to know

Fail to grow

Sharing themselves with random females each week

Conversantly secure with repeated sins

Justified and feeling fine within a society that endorses poor male
actions

Ignorant to self-reflection

That's what's happened

When the depths of society, culture and global constructs prophesizes

that your un-thoughtful male behaviour carried less of an impact and is
somewhat acceptable

Your worth is now questionable

However, one forgot to question the measuring of self-value

Whilst disregarding the narratives of what society deemed okay or
acceptable

Sexual tranquillity and it's sharing of frequencies which is transcended
via the exchange of sexual physicality

Is also to be looked at ambiguously

Do not believe that a man is immune from the various energy's that he
engages with

One will eventually feel drained when his body continues to be given

Shared with multitudes of women

Scattered across locations

Everybody walks with his vibrations

His energy is loose with no concentration
Energy is a powerful entity
Patriarchy said you win
However, you're shared being
And your shared energy
Means you're far from wholesome
Sexism failed to give you a narrative
When you began to reflect within self upon thee beyond 'he'
One must look at themselves beyond the gendered nouns and more so
the pronouns where sexual vulnerability is concerned
It's clear that a man must understand themselves first if they want a
'good woman'
However, ladies..... this understanding works both ways

Laughing To My Friends

Hi Mrs Whoever
We're chilling
Don't let my female presence fool you
Tell your mum I don't want to marry you
Tell your dad your son does what I do
I smartly do what I want
Running into an old interest like what was his name again?
Laughing all the way to my friends
Daddy said women will always have options
And well….I never ran out of any
They say behind every man is a strong woman
Well, behind every solid daughter is also a strong woman
I just replicated this
And became a boss through E.E.B.M in time

Ladies You Have Estrogen Supremacy

Why have one?

When you can have more

One two three four

She can have them all

Testosterone made this easy for you

She's got options

Go head

Explore this

Reckless

I care

But tonight, I don't

So, don't ask me to be me

Because I won't

So tonight, I'll have a reckless life

Spilling my drink and my minds heavy with a light high, like a rolling stone

And I can't answer my phone

My communication became barren as I laugh with strangers that I don't even know

Pass that percentage

The higher the numeral the better

Bottles got this crowed feeling lose and untethered

Tunnelled path to the ladies so I can get myself together

Q & A time

"Should we do another one?"

A slur of words mouth "Ahh go on let's do it!"

Like the legendary Michael Jackson song SCREAM

Forget sanity I don't want to be sane

This liquid filters through my zest

There goes that fire on my chest

Transitioning into a ...

Wait

Fingers up to regrets

Let's share the hazy stuff

Me next

With an absorption of intoxicated breaths

Exhaling sleepy stress

I'm gone ....
Until I wake up with a hangover
And forget what's gone on

*Passions of A *******

Let me gaze at you
Admiring our silhouette together
Whilst I sit on top of you
Stand over there
Let me admire you
Handsome eyes as I gaze at you
Let me tell you how much I want you
Streaming my affection all over thee
A wrath of intimacy traded for divined security
Let me give this to you
Brainless when around you
An intoxication of lost thoughts
A thrill seeker turned sinner
Our presence shouldn't be here
No need for resistance
This chemistry makes us feel like winners
Come one step closer
Let me caress you
Looking after you comes easy
Come over here
Let me do what a woman supposed to do

Spilt Milk

On a high from being reckless
I need my ego massaged
So, I'll be free with no regrets
I don't live for the moment much
But if I do, let me cover the atmosphere black

So today I'm far from kind
Your attraction gives you deceitful eyes
My ego is empowered by your lustful desires
Thus, subsequently changing the position of patriarchy within your
presented disposition
Due to your lustful transition
Top of the food chain and so I will eat what I want
You're first....
But only in my time
She's in control
Synonymously shifting the power constructs
Now this is feministic patriarchy at its finest
All masculine energy became mortal
Weak when around she
Testosterone VS Estrogen
Your misogynistic ways always fall victim due to your hormonal needs
And so, she capitalises on your lack of self-control
Men.....................
This is too easy for me

Bring the drugs and I will bring the flame
Bring your desires and I'll bring you my passions

Give me your body let me abuse it
But If u ask for my heart
I'll give you my juice of selfish silence
Silencing the element of your care
But you said you was a M.A.N
You said men's poor sexual actions was justified as its just their
biological make up
As it hurts more when a woman does wrong
But you can move on
You're a man
Multiple sexual engagements does not affect men
You can engage and not always be emotionally attached or impacted
as much…. right?
So
M.A.N up!
And stop with all that estrogen emotions stuff when she does you
wrong
Or when you lose her
And, enjoy your lonesome house
Crowded with a selection of temporary women

Stop all that stuff
Big boys don't cry
That's women's stuff right
So, M.A.N and move on
Spilt milk…. here's a rug
You clean it

WOMAN
E.E.B.M

Never underestimate the strength of a woman
Never underestimate the strength of a mother
Keeping all things in harmony together
Exampling her words through courage and the art of loving
They are amazing
She's amazing
E.E.M.B .....she's simply remarkable

Scribbled

Yeah, sure poetry can be seen as an expression through words
Which is the embodiment of one's mind
Yeah, sure poetry is an advocate for us to share our experiences,
knowledge, and messages to those who wish to read
Zarra's ideology of poetry: A poetic language communicating passions
through a visionary of letters
But the truth is... 'MY' poetry captures the different corners of
well....you're reading it right
So, you know what?
Poetry is not all about being deep and solidifying whatever it is I or you
are explaining
So, I will write irrelevant poetic nonsense because that's real
That's heart
That's poetry
That's no f**** given
So don't forget the fun in poetry
Because language is the dialogue of knowledge
And language is powerful
Let me share mines with you

Poker Face

Play the game

Hello change

Don't be surprised when faces don't stay the same

How many around you will appear the same when they are out of your view?

You can't count on others of whom you don't go home to

Loss of honesty

Blending in with society's teens

Coercively fitting right in

Don't blame me, he, or she

Blame thee

Point the finger

Now you're twining with everyone else who looks in the mirror

And your quantity of 'share' slipped through your fingers and onto the common floor

No need for the word care

The darts are here

Take a shot

Bullseye!!!

Your loyalty disappeared

Let the beast be released

Black eyes for the ones that are in your way

Because there in 'your way'

Deflect the truth

Don't tell them it's really you

Do as they do

Walk on the surface of other beings

Embody self-righteousness

Argue your way first

Be ignorant before you become compliant

Forget self-reflection or accountability

It's better to argue, no such words as respect, honour or sorry

Its best to hold a grudge

Its best you remain right

Its best to live in conflict

Its best to appear right even when wrong

Better to live like this than to reason

Don't let them see that you were wrong

You don't need to admit fault

Who are they to make you feel belittled?

Plus, your faults weren't as bad as theirs

That's right

Because your right

Because you've been through the struggle and willing to get it by any means

And you could say sorry

But just make sure that you follow it up with a justified excuse

Ohhh look how pride and ignorance is a killer

I didn't say this behaviour was right

I didn't say it was just

I'm just saying that this pretentiousness and lack of honesty is the bedrock of our society

It's a dog-eat-dog world

Sleep

Just don't expect good energies to sleep with you

Why So Serious?

S*** went left
But you know the saying
It is what it is
So, f*** it
Have fun with it

Emojis

It was always about the laughter

Live, laugh, be immature, act a fool, have fun

Enjoy the good and the bad

Enjoy the moments when you feel happiness and when you felt sad

Even when others have done you wrong

Its fine!

Laugh

It's done now

It was only a day, a month, and a year

It was always an experience

It was always there for you to laugh through

Sign Here

A sense of self-worth on a pedestal that only those with an artistic
mind
Who stand for justice
Speak with honesty
Disregard their own pride and ignorance
Attain fearless courage
Appreciate the care from others
Value love and equality
Seek for understanding and peace above everything
Can be placed as my counter parts

Enable me to deconstruct the saying of
'Children must be seen and not heard'
Great minds continue to prevail in any space
Strength, with the quest to know more
Strength, with the quest to go left when others go right
Fearless to say "no"
When most would say they might
These people are an anomaly
Use acceptance to socialize with them
Such a tough quality to acquire
Only acceptance will enable people to accept those of whom are
different to them or choose not to conform
Be patient
And wait to see the beauty from the youth of whom are different to the
rest
As a wise person will have more questions than answers
.......Teach them

No man is worse than a woman and no woman is worse than a man
Lack of growth
Closed minds
Well, they could never understand certain retaliations
Glad people finally got there
This entire book illustrates mines
A teenager started this book
I've been awake since I arrived
I've just been waiting for people to wake up in time
Arrogant: signature signed

Chapter 3

Dedicated to the Love Anthem

"Watch how the universe generates when love is present because love is an energy" *(Z, Hitsburg)*

Introduction

The equilibrium between love and society has always led me to think about the type of attachment that we can form with others especially when in unison with each other and this is not to be mistaken for only romantic relationships with a spouse but also the relations that we can form with family and friends etc and how this cohesion of people and feelings can unite a community of people.

When I decided to write about the theory behind 'Dedicated to the Love Anthem' I wanted the understandings to be more expansive than just 'loving relationships' as there is more to love than romance. In doing so, this chapter breaks down love lost in society and how the energy of love can be much more universal between people. Therefore, I have related the component of love in parallel to universal systems including governmental systems and constructs, oppression, and overall society as it clear that the elements within love; in focus of society and overall civilization is intensely missing. Thus, causing factors such as crime, oppression, abuse, and poverty etc to be so prevalent in history and during today's current times thus causing a rise in mental health conditions more so now than in previous generations.

My theory behind Dedicated to the Love Anthem focusses upon love lost within society and how the energy of love can be universal but more so how the element of care for others has started to become obsolete, resulting in an individualistic society as opposed to integrated society. Therefore, this chapter investigates in greater detail by examining how society has transformed the way in which people need and value the entity of love, whilst also exploring how the mental strain in relation to the cognitive fear to financially acquire luxury goods and a basic standard of living has intensely impacted upon people's priorities and efforts to attain and sustain love in contrast to this.

This chapter continues to explore how social media has impacted upon the way people communicate and how this has also impacted upon the longevity of relationships within society. Lastly this chapter continues to explore how the loss of previous generational gender roles and domestic tradition has impacted upon the number of people entering long lasting romantic couplings due to the shift of blurred values between people's new 21st century expectations within gender roles and how this generational shift of new values, expectations and responsibilities has caused a confusion within todays younger generations views regarding domestic labour such as household duties and domestic leadership regarding which gender does what role domestically and financially. Finally, this chapter concludes by analysing the power of love.

I know when most people hear of the word 'love' most will believe that I am directly referring to the love of romantic relationships between spouses, however there is more to 'love' than just the love we give to a partner. Love is a lot of things, and it is very much a subjective topic regarding people's individual experiences, views, morals, values, and understandings etc within love to which I always say is great! As our differences within how we see love is one to be understood and the vibrations of our differences of opinions can create a great cohesion of understandings from one person to another thus creating harmony; as no one person is wrong or right within their experiences of love per se, it's just one to be understood.

Love is a lot of things, but love has an incredibly great deal to do with self. The transparency behind the smoke is that love primarily centres towards how a person loves and lives within the principles of themself mentally and physically. Which would dictate their own domain and energy and what they expect from themselves regarding how they live within their own principles and how they generally choose to live their lives. This in theory, would indicate that only the person at hand has the power to develop their own growth, create their own principles and choose how they handle conflictual situations. Because bad actions, lies, lack of accountability, dis-respect, guilt and more should affect themselves first before anybody else and/or spouse when at fault. A principle of self does not mean that people will not make mistakes however, it does help to enable a growth factor to take place in relationships when the bare faced transparency of honesty is verbally actioned by both persons.

To truly love another, one must mix the various components of kindness, thoughtfulness, respect, accountability, responsibility, listening, care, commitment, loyalty, trust and always honesty, plus so much more. Embracing a love ethos would mean that people utilize all dimensions of love in it is entire entirety. This would help to give people a different way of living with themselves and then secondly with others, possibly helping to create unity. As love is more than a joyful feeling because as listed above it takes more than just 'love' to be able to love. Therefore, when merging the entity of love in parallel to society's everyday social functioning's, one must view love as not purely the factors of a sensual or romantic love but more so transform love into what I call a 'love ethos' as this would enable people to act upon the elements within love when integrating with strangers in everyday socialization thus converting love into a principle of practicality within how we approach, communicate and socialise with each other, with a hope that these ethics will create more kindness to be present not only in our personal relationships but also in the world.

However, in reality most people live in capitalist society which does not endorse the ethos of love in everyday socializations as people are slowly becoming much more engrossed upon the strive to financially acquire goods. To continue, with western society becoming a much harder functioning for people to become a financial success and resulting in the bare necessities of life becoming much harder for people to acquire and to sustain an adequate standard domestic lifestyle due to the ever changing financial economic systems of inflation, taxes, and consumerism rising each year, making it harder for new generations to be financial stable thus causing new generations and individuals in general to therefore become more concerned with their external goods as a pose to their internal needs.

In conclusion it may be argued that people in the modern era are therefore less concentrated on the compassion and kindness to give to others let alone practicing a love ethos. Though, if people are more

72

concerned with mass consumption when purchasing more and more luxury items for external gratification as opposed to gaining internal growth (by developing and understanding themselves as a person), then mass consumerism will continue to increase mass production, resulting in mass destruction to the individuals' conscious development.

Love Vs Society

When we look at the component of love in relation to the worlds current state of affairs including obscurity, poverty, racism, immigration, capitalism, mental health, poor democracy, and epidemics and much more; you begin to see the true state of the worlds injustice and how much people have become a commodity to the money that they earn. As centuries manifest and as society develops, the craft to attain the basic humanistic necessities such as shelter, food and usage of affordable transport has become much harder to afford and/or acquire than in previous years and previous generations due to forever changing economic global systems. Individuals struggle to grasp upon the basic foundations that cater towards a happy and comfortable life and good wellbeing has now become the main strife that individuals in the new age society place their effort, tenaciousness, and integrity into.

As a result, individuals in today's 21st century may have become much more concerned with the need to provide themselves with a comfortable standard of living as the acquisition of these necessities have now become much more mentally harder to gain and/or maintain due to those in position of power creating systems of economical oppression via the regulation of the global economy and man-made debt and so forth. In which as a result has consciously forced people to live in fear once sub servantly forced to fear living under the breadline of financial instability. In parallel to this, it can be argued that the power of supreme systems of oppression has had an impact upon people's cognitive processes thus sub consciously transforming the way in which human relations merge with each other and more so upon how people value one another, possibly changing the art of love and care for others. To explain, it can be debated that individuals within todays current generations have become more fearful of losing financial luxury's such as cars, houses, general wealth, expensive goods, luxurious clothes, exclusive electronic devices and so forth thus purely because it is now much more harder to acquire and attain these luxury items than it was in previous generations; likewise the 'mental strain' it puts on an individual to attain such goods has become the nucleus to keeping society in a cross circular chase to acquire wealth above everything and everyone. When we take a closer look at the human brains cognitive behaviour in relation to its regular functioning; once focused on a desired goal such as in this case it is the continuous need to gain financial wealth; it becomes more transparent that it is the element of 'fear' that has been used as a tool to mentally oppress, de construct and ultimately transform the mental cognitive thought processes of others within society. This mental strain of fear may have shifted peoples personal values and efforts when merging and socialising with others. And it is this very mental strain to acquire more and more that people are under, which has contributed to the many factors as to the increase of mental health across adults and young people. However, it could be contested that this rise in mental health is of no surprise and very much evitable as mental health and suicide was never something that was new, it always apparent however society at current is much more open to the discussing the troubles and struggles that people face now as appose to previous generations. One can only see the rise in the attempt to break the stigma attached to mental health as a positive cause for change as

74

this is helping others to seek help and helping people to become much more sympathetic to the turmoil and struggles that people go through and so I must strongly highlight that in my own opinion this is a step in the right direction in order to helping others within our personal social relations and for society at large.

To summarise: the more global economy's year by year puts financial debts upon society therefore increasing the stress on the everyday working person by increasing the general financial costs upon the necessities of living i.e., house, cars, childcare fees, this results in life its self-becoming much more stressful for people to build a comfortable life than in comparison to previous generations. These above discrepancies may have enabled the entity of love to be lost within society, resulting in people not upholding their appreciation for others and therefore leading love to possibly becoming a sabotaged attachment within a person needs, priorities, and values due to the mind being over saturated with the stress to financially gain. When this happens, it may create a character too focused on the externalisms in life and possibly left feeling un-fulfilled and always in search of more external gratification.

Love Vs Social Media

In the 21st century society, mass influence (both consciously and sub consciously) is heavily transferred through the platform of social media thus revolutionising the way in which people love and communicate, to which it may have caused great communication globally, but it has also caused a lack of communication socially. Therefore, generations may now need to verbally communicate much more intricately with a spouse if wanting to build at least half as much of a strong relationship to their previous predecessors'. However, if social media is the new format of communication, then verbal communication can become despondent. Therefore, the lack of ability to physically communicate within society may also impacted upon loving relationships within society due to people lacking the ability to communicate in all levels of verbal communications thus possibly impacting upon individuals forming romantic relationships.

The blurred lines of social media communication may again mean that the new aged relationships will have to communicate much more transparently about their own values and where and how they place their values as a man, woman, or person within their daily lives. Because no longer are relationships easy to sustain due to the blurred lines of communication within social media and due to the loss of traditional values within society, meaning there I no blue print to follow. It can be argued that the culture of social media has transformed people's level of communication, values and reality whilst adversely increasing vanity, consumerism, unrealistic expectations, and disposable relations all of which can develop a shallow mindset and creating an 'individual society' within civilisation.

In summary, the full diaspora explained within this segment between romantic relationships, the normality of social media and its transformation within communication and its impact on people's personal values; may have contributed to the energy of love in the world is now a lot harder to acquire, build and sustain due to revolutionary platforms of influence.

Superficiality Vs Values
When highlighting the entity of 'fear' as a tool; once external used as a

76

mechanism to advocate a constant cognitive strain to acquire, it leaves uncertainty open to question if the narrative of this constant cycle to attain goods is the possible fore frontal target of individuals new constructed personal goals and priorities. Moreover, subsequently impacting upon the new age individuals' level of personal morality, integrity, and their values regarding what people in the 21st century consider to be meaningful to them in relation to their hierarchy of needs, personal values, and principles when faced with the constant need for more and more. Leaving one question in what position do people in society 'practically' place their level of love and care for others? let alone a romantic relationship and none the less how moralistically do they live with themselves if only concerned with the things that impact them and not others?

In general terms it can be argued that the everyday modern persons values and priorities are now changing, with an open conception that people have now become much more concerned with the need to attain expensive/external luxuries above the luxury of love.

Overall due to the physical and mental stress that it takes to acquire luxury goods and a basic standard of living, this can result in some individuals wanting to hold on to luxury items over holding on to a relationship due to the constant effort it takes to acquire external goods than in comparison to love itself. All of which could create individuals to be inductors of 'greed' which could help to transform into selfishness, with the only thought to continue to acquire more items than one may actually need and possibly more concentrated and concerned with self before anybody else, even when others around them may need help as opposed to being left alone. The above understandings clearly do not apply to all people however, it is a heavy factor to highlight when questioning society's current state of affairs where wealth, poverty, mental health, racial and social divisions, and lack of unity is concerned.

One must state there is nothing wrong with looking out for self, in some dynamics were forced to look out for own safety and happiness though it can become concerning when others do not recognize or do not help others of whom may also be in need. The elements of selfishness and greed is what has created the 'dog eat dog' phrase of which we are all aware of as ultimately it is governmental systems such as institutions, laws, legislations, and organisations etc to which we have been placed under to survive. Subsequently, creating an overall societal environment that synonymously thrives under the usage of fear, greed, and selfishness for individuals to live under, leading to the phrase of 'dog eat dog' to become more apparent within social functioning's when needing to survive in a world that inhibits 'self'.

Nevertheless, a person's environment is only one factor when analysing the elements of selfishness and greed and if a persons has been born into financial privilege or financial poverty. The conditions a person grows up in can contribute to how people see the word 'care' and whether if they are a product of their environment. However, with this highlighted, one must also pay attention to the biology within a person's character traits that a person is born with to which will also remain a strong factor towards a person's personality and development. In addition, this is not to exclude other factors which shape a person's ability of care for others, as we know a person's culture, religious beliefs and parental rearing would have all had its impact upon a person's ability to care for others. To debate: some people may say that some people are just born that way and so would have always lacked certain qualities. Whereas some may argue that it is a person's environment which can dictate a person characteristics and personality. All of which hold great sufficient value to the underlaying question at hand in that:

Are People Born Greedy and Selfish? Or is it society's economic functioning or a person's local environment which dictates a person's character? One can only contest that all factors are valid. This leads me on to mention the opposition between nature Vs nurture, both of which hold valid impacts upon a person's development and character.

To conclude, it can also be argued that the value of romantic love has possibly becomes of lesser importance to the modern-day individual's hierarchy of needs than in contrary to previous generations. Thus, because overall the acquirement of love itself comes with less effort, craft and mental despair and can be seen more so as luck or a blessing to receive, in which people may not generally value the things they cannot see.

The bedrock of our humanistic outerisims and need for love, support, unity, and wellbeing begins to possibly become of less significance, thus adversely subsidising the 'ethos of love' socially and personally and therefore causing a lack of love in society. One must intensity question if a persons need for a romantic love only comes at a later age in life, if love itself was ever an importance to them to begin with? When the blessing of love can come at any age in life. Of course, most would criticize my narrative on 'love lost within society' to not be the issue. However, when we take a moment to decipher the contrast between fear, love and society in reference to how much people have somewhat been forced to strive for goods as appose to striving for the care of others, then it can only be contested that love is only high on peoples 'personal' needs and not within their need for social unison i.e., such as how often does a person share respect and give love to others in general when being an everyday citizen i.e. helping a mother with her pram, offering help to a person who looks lost on their travels, giving help to the homeless and much more. This may mean that the element of care for all people within society at large may become an act that becomes scarce, uncommon, and subjective because the 'fear' of suffering from poverty and the stresses that financial instability brings; may begin to take more importance in a person cognitive thought process. If a person's mind is consumed with financial gain over helping others, then capitalism as a function will prevail by shaping how a person functions and socialises with strangers and with people in general within their daily functioning's. An individual's thought process of acquiring more and more will have a detrimental effect on civilisations social functioning because the bigger picture is that capitalism will continue to triumph, leaving the acts of care and freedom to become sabotaged. If people are placing their strife to acquire more as their main target, then the acts of kindness when integrating with strangers and people in general will be of less importance therefore resulting in the act of care to become near obsolete within society.

The pressure to attain a basic stable life has had an impact upon society in every dynamic possible because once we trade love for the acquirement of luxury goods, one's ability to hold on to their integrity for the sake of others or a relationship can become resolute. The reasons explained above could all contribute towards a plethora of deducted socialisms both societally and personally. The loss of genuine socialisms could contribute to a loss or decrease in a person's integrity to sustain long-term relationships with spouses, increase disposable relationships, remove people from creating foundations, decrease a person's personal confidence, and contribute to the lack of societal unity (plus much more). Lacking genuine socialisms could result in an increase of one parent families, social division, artificial confidence and an increase in poverty and mental health. This leads me on to mention that whilst societal financial pressure has intensified, it may have also simultaneously sabotaged peoples true need for love and may have undoubtably placed even more intense pressure onto the 21st century man to provide (for those who wish to) or to be seen as a man of wealth.

Moving forward, it is transparent that ultimately the way people live their lives and the gendered roles that people were once positioned under has changed. This is a great transition of change within individuals personal and outward freedoms and therefore the new 'normal' or whatever society considered to be normal is now subjective to each person, none the less this is a great transformation of change. However, it is also to be accepted that whilst we are momentarily in a transition of societal change, it is also actualisation that previous gendered traditions and its gendered roles will still take a while for these domestic expectations and roles to be dismantled. Leading to some individuals to continue to uphold traditional values such as placing men as a provider and the woman as the care giver. Nonetheless within today's modification of change it is now not only men who feel the pressure to provide but also women, with a scoop that men's value to provide has only intensified for those of whom still uphold traditional values and therefore position themselves as the domestic provider. Although, due to societal shifts in gender roles, it can be strongly debated that for a man to be a provider in this current age, is now much more of a choice as appose to a given responsibility than in comparison to previous generational men. Leaving one to question: Do men in today's current generation have less domestic responsibility than those in previous generations?

Traditional Values of Gender Vs Modern Values of Gender
The production of capitalism and the supremacy of patriarchy has had

the greatest impact upon how gender has been represented and valued due to social construction and its assumptions of female and male's 'natural' biological abilities and proposed skills to be defining factors of employment. When analysing capitalism as a by-product to the financial division of labour, it becomes clear that capitalism has also constituted to the functioning of patriarchy. For example, some industries of work historically aligned their salaries in line with females and male's biological characteristics. As a result, this then created the labelling of some working positions to be considered as either feminism work or masculine work. The labelling of gender within employment also contributed towards a patriotic society with males geared to financially gain more money than their female counterparts in certain industries of work. And if money is power then men had a higher status quo over women and power therefore enabling men's voices and opinions to have carried more importance over women's economically and sociably. Resulting in males to be more financially powerful both economically and domestically i.e. All of the above subsequently resulted in the battle of the sexes, with woman previously forced to live submissively under a man's lead thus resulting in the lack of gender equality, value, opportunities, and respect and causing various ramifications between gender, financial gain and status quo in relation to power. Ultimately constituting to the oppression of women through economic capitalism. To explain, the ability to work for a living and generate an income as a main bread winner creates power within a household for whom holds the leadership position theoretically speaking. In previous generations this was a position held by the man for the philosophical narratives within biology, therefore putting females at a disadvantage financially, domestically, and sociably. However, let's not forget patriarchy was created for men to sustain power over his male competitors and whilst sustaining economical empire. Moving forward, the transformation of

82

various societal changes in relation to gender had generated protests to take place in society, with women activism taking place in search of gender equality to which has all contributed to the 'new normal' to become existent in today's society. However, fast forward into today's current times then it can be debated that as gendered equality continues to be distributed in all areas within society's functioning, that it may have also led to a few blurred lines within today's current generations domestic roles and responsibilities. We shall investigate this further within the next few chapters.

One can only critique the historical feminist movement by stating that it was the attribute of 'appreciation' which was what was missing in previous generations domestic roles and household responsibilities. Hence women's drastic drive for gender equality due to feeling taken for granted and belittled by their husbands. One must highlight that both the man and the women's domestic roles are to be appreciated and are equally of great value when raising a family and even more so upon how they live with each other as a couple. However, once appreciation is lost, drastic change will take place resulting in the 21st century woman now learning and mimicking the actions of their male counter parts both professionally, socially and within romantic relationships. Causing a shift of status quo and possibly threatening the man's position in the household, with some men stating that society is attempting to emasculate them. However, in contrast to this, some men are in favour of the above gender changes due to possibly seeing the man's responsibilities as one they no longer need to live up to. Leaving various social media platforms to discuss the value of men and women into days 21st functioning and how and what determines gendered value if any? Once again communication will be key for the current generations when attempting to build a relationship with another person as there is no one way model to replicate.

The New Normal Vs Mr and Mrs's

The world we know as of today is very much different than in previous centuries with digital technologies continuing to revolutionise the world in all aspects. However, people's attitudes regarding old ideologies of domestic roles, labour work and domestic leadership is still under transformation. Purely because when people hear of a 'stay-at-home dad' some may still have a raised eyebrow. Though with this transformation of domestic roles in transition, it can be contended that in today's day and age of change it has caused a confusion between the roles that men and women deliver within relationships that we co-exist in today's current times. Therefore, the old constructed traditional gender roles still underlyingly exist within some of today's heterosexual relationships attitudes. Traditional gender roles and its responsibilities still synonymously impacts upon the roles within all relationships of today irrespective of sexuality. Some people may believe that they are dismantling the oppression of gender roles by using their own freedom of choice. However, relationships are still impacted by historic gender roles, thus purely due to some individual's stagnant attitudes of whom still find it odd when gender roles reverse such as woman asking men to marry them, men leading upon child care duties, women being the bread winners within the house hold an so forth. If one finds this odd or something to which raises an eyebrow then it is clear, that old traditions still have an impact upon the roles women and men cater to in society both domestically and professionally. Society may have changed however people's attitudes possibly not as much.

However, the new normal is whatever people want it to be now. With the abandonment of gender roles and the increase of women's financial equality thus creating more independency for women, in contrast the 21st century man may now have two possible dispositions where the households functioning is concerned. For example, firstly: men of today possibly face more intense pressure to be the main bread winner due to women's increased financial equality, therefore giving men more employment competition. In contrast to this, secondly: it can be heavily debated that the modern day man may in actuality experience less pressure to be the main bread winner, again due to women acquiring financial equality in society therefore possibly reducing or threatening the need for male domestic leadership. To expand, as a result it can be contended that women are not only continuing the role as the mother (for those who have children respectively) but she has also acquired a new role to financially be a provider therefore leaving men with less domestic responsibility than in comparisons to men in previous generations when it was frowned upon for women to work in certain industries or work period. Women's new work ethic may have possibly threatened the man's domestic value where both family and romantic relationships are concerned.

Overall, the new factors I've explained may have caused much more strain on relationships within today's times with some men becoming much more resistant to be embody the role of a provider, especially once the expectation for men to be a financial provider became of less significance to 21st century relationships and can instead be seen as negotiable or more of a choice. Subsequently, it is now clear that domestic leadership is now to be readdressed.

Weirdly, although some men positively endorse an integration of equality between the genders domestically and financially, some men (not all) may have used this societal change counter productively, by using women's economic development as an excuse not to place their efforts into becoming a financial provider for a spouse or family and therefore resisting domestic responsibility. Yet, may still expect domestic gratification, when expecting to be valued as a man of labour and therefore valued under the same merit to men in previous generations, despite not attaining the same work ethic, leadership and bearing of responsibilities in comparison to the men before them. The double standard of some men endorsing new gendered adaptations in society by supporting female equality or feminism and using this as an excuse to deliberately decrease their own financial responsibilities when in romantic relationship; yet, are still expecting to be valued and as a man of labour (which holds traditional values) cannot co-exist when discussing the meaning of what It means to be a man in today's modern times. Because if a man chooses not to part take in domestic leadership, but expects to be valued as a man, without openly stating that he is not a 'traditional man' then this duality of the contemporary man vs the traditional man when forming relationships will only incur possibly conflict, competition, bitterness, laziness, and more battles between the sexes.

And so, can it be questioned that if the 21st century man still expects to be seen as a man of 'value' during an ever-changing society and therefore within a changing family functioning, then the expectations of what a man is valued upon within today's modern society now need to be re addressed.

Moreover, due the 21st century women's new profound attitude and mimicking men's actions by dating multiple individuals at one time, it can be argued that men in this day and age are now dating women of who are mirror of themselves. Leading to men being much more reluctant to be chivalrous when dating women in threat of whatever it is that annoys them about this. It Is clear that the 21st century woman is role reversing dating irrespective of sexual positioning. The threat that ladies no longer put all of their eggs into one basket when dating, seems to have threaten the modern man's confidence, pocket or whatever else it may be. Causing men to possibly have the same insecurities when dating, which woman once used to have. Due to this, some men may have begun to use chivalry as a weapon to deduct romance when approaching women or being in relationships with women overall resulting in chivalry to be a despondent act of the pass.

At current, not only is the woman continuing to historically deliver upon her role as the mother to her child/children, she now also obtains the pressures of her male counter parts when providing for her family (especially if she is a single parent respectively) by having to financially provide and continue to take care of the domestic responsibilities in the house. Due to this duality of roles, it can be argued that the 21st century mother not only bares the stresses of a woman but also of the man. However, with the rise of women's new attitudes such as the *'I don't not need a man attitude'* is this not the price she pays? Therefore, the new shift within parental roles in the cross context between provider and nurture regarding motherhood and fatherhood and how these integrate exclusively, could create new distress on romantic relationships thus resulting in a possible increase of co-parenting in today's current times.

In summary, sociology's theories regarding the family structure and functioning have been knocked and crunched due to the changes within modern society. Therefore, domestic family theory's such Functionalism and New Right ideologies no longer hold precedence in today's 'normal' family functioning due to the rise of Feminism theory and Marxist family theory becoming much more apparent in today's family functioning. As the world becomes much more far removed from religious value's; it has now entered in to a more secular society. This is possibly another factor regarding why society or some individuals do not attain intense values or virtues of humility and gratitude or elements of principles, reflection, accountability, honesty (to say the least) and overall are less likely to value people, appreciate or value the act of love. All of which, may be another reason as to why most individuals may only see the value of love and marriage once reaching an older age and not in their junior or young adult years due to a loss of religious values or spirituality at the least.

Old Generation Expectations VS New Generations Expectations

To continue, the lack of gender roles and tradition within today's times may have possibly caused heterosexual couples to become allot more somewhat confused when having to decide upon who plays what role in the household, who looks after the children, who is the domestic bread winner, who does the DIY chores around the household and the overall domestic labour within the household. To which these discrepancies and confusion may have filtered into the expectations and standards upon what it means to be considered a 'man' or 'woman'. Overall society and the media may have influenced and transformed the way in which people couple. Leading to a discrepancy between the lack of cohesion between values and gender roles, to which this lack of domestic cohesion may have filtered between 'expectations and standards' regarding what people define or view a woman or man to be. This causes great conflict or confusion within relationships but also upon how men and women integrate romantically when courting and attempting to function as a couple. For example, a person who attains more modern values but may have merged with a traditionalist person may face discrepancy within their relationship which will need to be addressed because both person domestic beliefs have been shaped differently and this will continue to show up in their relationship if not communicated. If not communicated, then these discrepancies may

88

lead to domestic confusion leading people in the 21st century failing to see eye to eye when entering new relationships. Resulting in people finding it much harder to couple in this generation. The possible confusion between gender roles and domestic expectations may have an impact upon the number of heterosexual couplings longevity suffering because of this duality and its conflict of interest.

Do not get me wrong I state that there has been both positives and negative outcomes when eradicating the tradition of gender roles. As this has contributed to women no longer facing 'justified' gendered oppression i.e., male misogyny, sexism and having to accept poor male actions in relationships. Instead, are now having much more rights politically, financially, socially, and economically (and various other areas of equality). However, if the loss of gender roles has enabled positives outcomes for women, in contrast it has also weighed heavy on this current generations ability to enter romantic relationships as mentioned before.

Nothing is wrong with domestic change and so the benefits of this change enforces peoples to have more free will and movement within their relationship, regardless of sexuality and this is to be considered an example of positive change. If a woman or man wants to uphold any role within their relationship i.e., a man being a stay-at-home parent and the woman being the breadwinner then this is far from a problem as long as both people have communicated upon what they want and how they want to formulate within their own family dynamic. However, for those heterosexual people of whom still uphold traditional values and would like to apply traditional roles within their own relationship; then this could cause a cross confusion between what men want and what women within their personal relationships.

Regardless, may it be old or new domestic roles and expectations that people attain or disregard; all agreements can be made within relationships, to which best suits both persons involved, as long as a positive balance, a mutual respect and always appreciation for what the other person contributes within the relationship (heavily missing in previous generations) has been communicated and implemented.

Moving forward, if people are becoming less tolerant to double standards or with woman having a new attitude of independence when dating who they like without the care of sexist views and lastly with men not liking women of whom mirror their own actions. Then this may result in there being less committed couples within society and if there are less committed relationships present then there will be allot less love in society and if there is allot less love within society then there will be more co-parenting, with some children (not all) being brought up in broken families. Such as possibly growing up with animosity for one absent parent or sometimes both parents, and with some children not receiving a peaceful love due to being raised by a broken parent.

In conclusion, all factors mentioned can or may dismantle a child's understanding upon what love is and what love looks like due to a lack of two parents in the household. This includes homosexual couples irrespective of sex and gender as all examples of love is important and valid when highlighting loving relationships between two people and how people function within relationships. If a two parented love is not exampled then it could possibly cause the child to struggle in loving another person in later life. This does not erode single parent's ethic, leadership, and diligence as a single parent. All single parents should be credited tremendously when raising a child on their own especially in today's current times and so take 'nothing' away from the single parents of who wake up every day to the responsibility of their child on their own. Singular parenting does not deter the child from growing up into a decent person and so I want to take the time to strongly state: much respect to the single parents working hard for their child/children, through their struggles that they continue to independently persevere through all battles thus for the love of their offspring, more credit to these parents as they are true superheroes in all forms.

Things happen and not all relationships will be forever and nor will relationships be perfect as they are not meant to be which is totally fine. Relationships are a constant grafting of compromises and sacrifices and so not all parents are able to stay together, people change, and people make mistakes. To continue, some people have children with others of whom they are not committed or love (or for various reasons) and sometimes people do initially date intentionally such as to begin a family and others did not mind having a child with the person they were with at the time etc and other reasons as each person's reasons for having a child is different, respectively. However as stated before things happened and no one or anything is perfect and nor do people get things right on the first go all of the time, we live, and we learn, and people can only hope that parents and people in general intentionally try to learn from all situations that they experience. However, things happen and sometimes children get caught in the middle of parental relationships. People make mistakes or make bad decisions; no parent is perfect which is fine and it is one to be understood. All parents can do is try to be honest, be accountable for their decisions and actions regardless of their parental age, try to remove their pride and be more intentional with whom they have children with or co parent with and lastly always do right by themselves and their child/children regardless what's happened with their previous spouse.

Moving forward when looking at the various factors between gender, roles, expectations, and standards it is no longer considered traditional or factual but more so defined from an individual perspective. As a result, this current generation is possibly under a lot more strain to hold more conversations around what they expect from each other as men and woman and as mothers and fathers. This could result in romantic relationships into days current society becoming tremendously more complex, fragile, harder to sustain and more difficult to become synchronised with another person's values in all realms than in previous generations due to the overall shift of gendered responsibility and with values now lacking clarity, not to mention peoples emergence for instant gratification. Possibly leading to the longevity of relationships becoming reduced and love for others in civilisation becoming in jeopardy at the hands of an individualistic society.

Individual Society Vs Integrated Society

The sabotage of love under wealth may result in western society having more individualism as appose social relations, less couples and marriages, less family units, and more co-parenting with an increase of disposable relationships. Despite science informing people physically and psychologically that human beings yearn for the attachment and affirmation of others.

If there is a decrease within attachment to others within populations due to the loss of a love ethos; with more people focusing on financial gain, this can and will increase the economic regulation of shallow consumerism enabling people to be more concerned with the goods that they own and how they financially appear to others. Once again it is open to debate if love lost within society has impacted within the love lost within romantic relationships and this includes homosexual relationships as ultimately love is love regardless of what gender or sex

92

is involved and so all persons irrespective of sexuality are under threat of falling victim to the loss of love. Furthermore, the loss of love and therefore the lack of care within society may and can impact upon people falling victim to anxiety and depression due to human beings personal phycological needs (more than sex alone) failing to be met which as a result can be a factor to causing a rise in mental health becoming even more of a global issue.

If we remove the ethos of love from out of this equation and look at the gradual changes within society, it becomes clearer that there is lack of communication within everyday socialisms thus causing less verbal and physical interactions with those in a person's local community or possible within our travels. A friendly chat with the customer service employee at the at the checkout tills has now become dormant due to self-service check outs becoming much more of an option (with some smaller stores only offering self-service check outs period) or the introduction of tap in debit/credit cards and the addition of tap in and out travel cards, phone apps. Resulting in shoppers/people to no longer need to communicate with staff employees to purchase goods, not to mentioned that we are also moving into a more cashless society as a functioning.

Therefore, it can be contended that we are moving into a more individualistic society however who will still give their time to give money to the homeless when society financially functions through more card transitions as opposed to solid money? Conclusively, physical communication in the 21st century can be seen as something that now needs to be done deliberately to have any kind of social interaction with other people, as the option of walking out of your front door and purchasing goods, travelling, and manoeuvring your way through the day can be done with no words crossed at all.

This leads me on to state: social media may have linked people to meet and speak with others globally, giving people exposure, a voice, an image, a platform, and an overall influence on global societies at large of which has positively impacted upon people's daily lives, well-being, and opportunities thus revolutionising the way people live their lives. However, in contrast, locally people are possibly much more individualistic within their daily lives, and with the decrease of face-to-face communication within our local communities due to social media apps keeping our attention (when bored, when waiting for the bus or train etc) it has adversely led to people having little integration with the people around them, of whom they pass on their daily commute etc. Possibly another reason why loneliness is a profound factor in today's civilisation within people's personal struggles as subsequently we may be communicating globally but not so much locally. It can be argued that social media is a possible illusion of reality and so the parallels between deception and true integration can become blurred thus interrupting people's judgment of morality (plus much more) when attempting to know the distinction between fact and fiction, valid information, and false information, who is honest and who is dishonest and overall, between a lie and the truth.

One can only sit back and view these confused disparities of deception as absolute absurd when the bigger picture to its confusion is that the element of care and love comes without a price and can be easily distributed to all of humanity thus for the aid of everyone, people, community, society, and nation. Therefore, it is important to give people the benefit of doubt as only the energy from the power of love can conclusively cure each person's loneliness, poverty, inequities, injustices, and inner turmoil.

94

The Power of Love

Love is such a powerful energy that it is utterly amazing when you authentically understand the depths of love in its entire entity. Love is very much subjective to one's principles, morality, values, and personal experiences and so there isn't a wrong or right 'perse' but only the conceptions of love and the combination of what it means to understand others.

The destruction but also the unity that love can create between one person to another, one group to another, one community to another thus enabling socialisms of romantic integration, national integration, community integration, cultural integration and global integration, thus uniting togetherness with people across the world... it is utterly amazing. Love is like its own oxymoron but more so an anomaly with different outcomes co existing in one space; it is like one coin but with two different sides between love and hate or more so love and fear and depending on what side is turned upside down it can generate either social unison or social divisions. Additionally, love itself can also orchestrate what we moralistically view as either good or bad.

Who ever said love isn't selfish, of course it can be but only for a moment. As it is only once a person takes the timeout to work, understand and love themselves can a person truly feel empowered within their own ability and energy to love another. Primary, once a person's self-love is present only then can they give this type of empowerment, support, and protection onto others and it is at that moment when the selfishness within love becomes shared because, they are then secondly able to give their synergy of love onto others.

To explain, once a person builds their own strength and creates their own self- love, which is formed from their 'primary core' of who they are, only then can these qualities then secondly be transferred onto others thus done out of care, compassion, and appreciation for those who they keep close or around them. Therefore, love can become draining, because to love another is to constantly give pieces of self (one's core) of which includes a person's vibrations, energy, positivity, communication, effort, mind, and physicality. And this is when love becomes powerful and it moves like an energy in the wind, generating it's light each time we try to do better by ourselves and others resulting in a unison of love and respect.

The impact that love can have on human beings can lead to desires, dreaming, foolishness, blindness, confusion, pain, loss, passions, craziness, strength, trust, respect, infatuation, euphoria, turmoil, war, hate, heartbreak and much more all felt due to the same entity of love itself. It is truly remarkable how one entity alone enables various impacts upon people; allowing one anomaly to spur numerous consequences of both negative and/or positive emotions with either good or bad outcomes, all due to one identical feeling felt. I say that the spirit of love is to give. Love is powerful. Let love win.

With mental health on the increase and the strive to acquire a comfortable standard of living being much harder to attain in today's current times than in comparison to previous centuries and with society being much more complex to live in more so now than compared to centuries before, it is only the vibrations of love that can give the energy to heal and cure all sufferings.

Dedicated to the Love Anthem the poetry has been written for all of the dreamers who enjoy romance, harmony, understanding, attachment, togetherness, frequencies, unity, fantasies, fairy tales, peace, and the simple things in life.

96

Dedicated to the Love Anthem
The Poetry

Dedicated to the Love Anthem Intro

Imagine words that speak to your heart
Imagine words that make you entwined with your own experiences
within love
Imagine the power of a united love
These are words that tell love stories
Do you want to be a part of a beautiful storey, filled with red and black
fantasies?
My words paint a picture that only an artistic love can see
Welcome to Dedicated to the Love Anthem part three

21 Backpacks

I journeyed towards the depths of love and left my generation behind me

Simply Love

Love is what love does
Love is the spirituality of which
Unravels the true meaning of reality

The Elements of Love

The three elements of love:

You're feelings for them

Your commitment to them

How you live with them

There is a lot more to this

Compromise: Because to love is also to give love even when we are resistant

Done for the love of self, others, teamwork, partnership, harmony, justice, and peace

Regardless, if were close, near or distant

Sometimes love is bigger than us

To love is to be fearless

To love is to have courage

To love is to have boundaries

To love is to give

To love is to attain humility

To love is to attain gratitude

To love is to be honest

To love another is draining

However, the rewards are a blessing beyond you

Be vulnerable to love, accept love and you'll know love

The Courage in Love

We all need real people around us
Someone to be loyal and respect us
That real conversation spoken of, just when we needed to hear it
That yearn for security when we are tired and insecure from the things
that displace us
That someone who gives us a sense of belonging
And affirmation to our beliefs when the odds are against us
That someone who fights for you when you feel lost and beaten
These are the real people that we all need around us
Appreciate the people who put you before themselves
As the courage to love hard in all its attributes
Is not something everyone knows how to give

A 70s Love

Call me a hippie
Cast me back to the 70s
Where the revelation was love
And the intoxication was weed
Because the high was always for peace

Something Like Love

Marriage, wants and needs

It's a funny old thing

You kind of have to be one those people that always dreamt of having a family, a foundation or valued it tremendously

If not

It might be something that just happened

Something you wanted because age was upon you

Something you seeked due to a place of insecurity

Or maybe because you finally got 'tired'

Plus, other somethings

But if it was never something that you placed as paramount or had a deep personal need for; with a positive longing for

A lack of something could say you may always want more

The Happiness of Love

Love is the most powerful energy
And happiness is the power of love
Without love there is no happiness
Without happiness there is no love
Both co inside with each other
Both energies won't exist without the other

Will

When your pain from hate is deeper than your will to love
Or your past has shaped you to attack when disturbed
Happiness will never be achieved
Harmony will never be allowed to breath
Peace will be in the distance and hard to see
Blinded pain has no site to walk forward towards peace

A Parents Love

Our parents are the first ones to make us feel love

So, let's teach love

So that we can hold on to love

So that we can give love

And keep the energy of love generating around the universe

Teaching our children that the essence of love is to be appreciated

Teaching our youth that love is a virtue

A Universal Love

What did you love this person for?
Because of a feeling...?
Was that just it.......?
So many others live a 21st century love
Thou only you can dictate the foundations of your love
Seek the depths of love in all its authenticity
A universal love never came easy
Be with someone who can help you to grow
As a person who can stimulate your mind
Is someone who will expand your growth and grow with you
Enjoy the challenges
Everything great needs time
Inhibit the integrity to preserve
Both good and bad emotions will play their role
Comprise when in disputes
Your attitude towards disagreements will be key
There's unity to your differences
There's peace to your vibrations
Only if your heart remains genuine
Only if your humility outweighs your pride
Only if you keep honesty near
Only if your aims and vision as a partnership is to become a stronger thee
Reflect upon your actions
Communicate with your spouse
Be open to criticism in order to seek a better you
Seek a relationship that will elevate you to be a better soul

Love VS Fear

Let love be your narrative

Let your love speak

And whisper an emotional bond of unity

Where these words tell a storey of togetherness

And you let yourself get lost in a sanctuary of two hearts, two minds in one world

Your desires heightening your intimacy

Be entwined with this feeling of imagination that can become your reality

And trust that happiness is all that you both need

The realism of it is, is that individuals are scared to let go and experience love without fear

You can create an illusion of overwhelming completeness

Though only if you both let go of yourself to feel this

Be fearless

Be committed

Be receptive

Be yourself

And one can make this type of love a normality

But only if you allow yourself to trust in love

Be responsible for your love

Believe in the power of love

Your love

One anticipated this

You know the vulnerability of bare souls

The same vulnerability that needs to be exchanged to another and wrapped with a ribbon of trust

In order to reassure the doubt of one's apprehensiveness

They said...

"I will take care of this"

Just like psychology within social relations that people yearn for each other and seek the security of others

Could you fulfil this need?

Let your love create a movement

A manifestation of fearless attachment to reach the levels of freedom

Tell them

Let us not think with our minds

Let us think with our hearts

And run away with life

Ultimately let's colour in all the gaps and have an animated love

One last thing...

The narratives of your storey will only exist if you let your heart speak

Selfish Love

A selfish love
Most would say a selfish love inhibits an egotistical person
Who only puts themselves first
A narcissistic character absorbed with oneself
Conceited: with only an interest upon all things regarding thee
Most would flee
However, let's put this selfishness into perspective
An intoxication of selfishness swirled with a balance of compassion and
a deep appreciated for others can be the art of....
Allow me to explain

When you truly know your worth
When you take pride in your worth
And you value love in its purest form
You will not or should not dehumanise others who value you
Because you will know what's good for.... you
Because they value who?.........you
Therefore, due to your strong sense of self worth
And your ego massaged when they make you a priority over anything
You will do anything to keep what you believe you deserve around you
And as selfish as its sounds
You will only want people around you who think of you first in
everything they do

When you know your courage
When you appreciate your own qualities
When you understand what you have to offer
And understand how you would like to live with others

Only then will you know what you want within your personal social relations
Only then shall you want the same partnership from those you keep close

Because once you know your worth
You shall then know the value of who you are
Once your understanding of 'self' is mixed in sync with the value of 'your love'
It is then that you'll genuinely want the best for you
Therefore, you begin to consciously give your love only to those who deserve you
Dilute a person's ego with their appreciation of love
This shall result into a selfish act to love
As the practicality of this cohesion will endeavour a person who wants to do right by you
Because they want to do right by themselves
Whoever said true love wasn't selfish
Of course, it can be
But only when you understand that self-love is the first step to a reciprocal love

The Physicality of Love

Imagine the physical power of love

And the essence of attraction, attachment, lust, intimacy, trust, and

emotions that you can feel all for one person and only because you let

them in

Into your mind

Into your happiness

Into your heart

Into your energy

The power of love is dangerous

Wouldn't it scare you to love someone so deeply?

It's honestly like handing someone a sharpened knife

So sharp that it glitters and then allowing your spouse to carve out your

heart

And grip it out with their bare hands

And there is a possibility that you could be left heartless

Or even heartbroken

All because you took a chance on love and gave one person the best

part of you

All because it felt right to

But here comes doubt

And so, you try to contain your feelings in fear of experiencing loves

pain

However, this synergy leads you to think...

What if they are the one who got away?

Hesitant with only yourself to blame

But your feelings don't feel the same

Do not let a good one get away

Love was always a risk
Exposing one's true vulnerabilities
But it is only the exchange of vulnerability which can birth ….trust

Feeling fulfilled when the earths waters connect to its shores
Exchanging vibrations of frequencies through the universes time
Enabling the suns energy of love to synchronise within you from inside
The feeling of love can be overwhelming sometimes
However, to love is also to be naked inside
You can run but your feelings can't hide

Like a book that you've read a thousand times
Or a novel that only your beloved can write the ending to
And you hope that they keep your feelings in their palms
And hold it tight with each rigid line
And never say goodbye

Imagine the intensity of butterflies that love brings
Do you feel it? did you feel it? did you feel the energy transferred each time you gave your loved one a kiss
Mix this transfer of energies with a person's passion, strength, trust, peace, and security
This shared mental space is ultimate tranquillity

You see
When this kind of love is reciprocal; and both lovers exchange their physicality
It is this physical transfer within a person's vibrations which enables energies to exist
It is that factor of unknowing control that you gave up when you let

love inside
You helplessly put down your defence as you couldn't help but feel
these emotions when you let yourself get lost in another person's life
It's amazing the type of control that you helplessly let go of when
you're in love
It is a powerful love when both people let go of themselves to give love

Loves Ambitions

When you become a commodity to the money you earn
When you realise that your societal being means nothing to systems of
supreme
You'll begin to realise who and what means more to you
When you realise what you want and more importantly what you need
You'll start to see those of no relevance fade away
Because they are not where you're at mentally so they could never
understand the outcomes that you're looking to achieve
Pretentious people and their social functions, fake conversations and
those who show case their material pieces, buttons, zips and the overall
sleek fittings to the clothes that fit you oh so well....... just no longer
moves you like it used to
When your hearts tired of the same old normalities of excitement
You feel different
You can put up that white flag
You're not afraid
You have the courage to strive for more now
As you no longer need to be summoned to wait until your bank account
says so
Roles reversed
Wages is your commodity now
They say be careful what you wish for
But this time you're ready for much more
No matter your goals
No matter the task
Be resilient
Time is needed
Every person has obstacles, issues, and struggles

No one person walking on this earth is walking perfectly
Walk with courage
For those who believe
Allow faith to walk under your feet
Your strength will be everything
However, the accountability of your actions, gratitude, humility,
support, and your level of honesty plus more, will be paramount to the
finish line that you hope you achieve
Because the bigger picture within loves ambition
Is how you loved
How you lived with self
And how you lived with others
The rest is up to you

She Said

Come here........
Let me look after you
When you've just finished a hard day's work
Let me ease your mind for you
Keep you relaxed, make you something to eat, simply chill with you
Talk to me, I'll free your mind whilst I lay with you
Hold you real tight
So that you know I'm holding on to you
Be that energy you need when all else has failed you
Give me your struggles and I'll try to take them away from you
Keep you stressed free
You can share this with me
And I will always try for you
I stroke your messy hair, look at you....
Your eyes are tired, your body is shattered but I still see perfection
when I look at you
And what is this all for?
Because I'm the type of partner
That makes it my priority to make sure that your ... by any means
That's my goal for you

Red & Black Fantasies

When the world gets too tough
And you cuddle up with me
And tomorrow just got a little bit easier to live
That's how I want my affection to feel
Like an overwhelming feeling of ease
I'll be that person
And just when you need an outlet to breath your there, your here,
you're with me
And you've waited so long to find who, to have this, to have us
And we are both in control of each other's hearts
And that's fine
Because I know you'll protect mines
Like warm water through one's fingertips
And smudges of lipstick I leave on your lips every time I give you a kiss
I want more nights like this
This type of connection will build a bond of unity
And one wrapped it so hard it's a part of you and me
You let down the barriers of fear to experience this and it was so easy
for you to do this
Because your shadow told you, that you'd safely be loved for you
And it would be effortless
So, go ahead
And let's create our own fairy tale and build a relationship that is
beyond the traditional and constructed normalities of life
And create our own power of love

Bring Back Love

Footprints towards your travel
A destination that is shared
You can get lost together and lose yourselves
And both can create a fantasy that only you and he/she knows
Your sacred place where both can bare, you're struggles, thoughts,
happiness, positives, laughter, fears, and edges of your pain
Where both will listen, and attempt to comfort each other's soul
An imagination of disillusioned security
Could you make this a normality?
Without our ability to dream how can we make this our reality
You can have an intangible, interchanging love that stays true to the
essence of fearless love
This is what the authenticity of love can bring
Using the 'being' of love as a verb as a posed to a 'noun'
You should then act upon love
It's a shame the way society has deemed love as a feeling of obscurity,
weak, and desperation
So, let's take the power of love back to what it is
Let's, bring back love
And not objectify your will to love and love itself as weak, shameful, or
soft
Because after all
To give and to receive love is the true power of happiness after all

He Said & She Said (Gold Sands)

He has all this love inside

She has all this love inside

He can't wait to share it with somebody

Shower them with his love, her love, no holding back, no hesitations

Just a free love who only let's go to give love

So, he can't wait to make a person feel special

And give them the feeling of security that they've never felt before

And even on her worst day, he will only look for her

And they will make each other smile

Her original love

His original love

One original love

With fun and arguments to be true

But this is perfect because she will always be real with you

They said

"Were stuck in reality with the struggles of the world

But we live like were in the fantasies of our minds"

And his blinded by temptation and the lust of others and so is she

That little bit of effort he will always make for her

She will give him his space when he needs time

She will let him be him

He wonders if he can make a person feel this way

She wonders if she can make a person feel this way

But he doesn't doubt his ability to love

Our generation of young people have lost the art of how to love

Love may have been cursed by polygamy

So, be old fashioned and have love like our parents once did
And when he's ready
And when she's ready to experience this type of love
They'll jump in together
Holding each other's hands as they sink into gold sands

Tunnel Vision

You should not ever want to hurt your loved one
So even when your mad
And near to hating them
A heart full of love can never be out weight by anything else
And so
You still see love tunnel visioned when you look at them
It's written that one should not opt for fury and wrath
As this is a sin
And with great rage comes great pain
But the power of love triumphs all
So even when your greatly mad
Love will heal the pain
But only if you choose to adhere to the virtue of humility

Why should you ever opt for fury and anger?
Without using your humility and strength to shun your pride
And come down to reconcile
As hurting them would only hurt you
The guilt would suffocate you from within
The insecurity of damaging her or him will only damage you

One should be committed and responsible for their actions in love
A reciprocal partnership of love, respect, and justice, this is just the
basic foundations of your mutuality towards each other as spiritual
human beings
You don't want to hurt them
Because you forever want to see happiness in their eyes when they look
at you

Their feelings are a reflection of your own
So, if one claims to love or be in love
Then, there should be no bigger feeling that could ever deter you from
opting to love their soul
You don't want to hurt them
Because ultimately one of your biggest fears is losing them

Queen of Hearts

One should love with every part of themselves, each fingertip, each hand, chest, arm, leg, body, soul
One should love until their mind doesn't think
And only their heart thinks, bangs, and beats
Circulating around you from your head all the way down to your feet
You should want to hold on to your spouse until you're breathless and you give them a great squeeze
You should want to hold on because you're entwined with how they make you feel
You should want to hold on because you need this energy and nobody else's
You should want to nurture them like a secret treasure
You should want to care for them when you're near, far, close and miles away
Just to show them..... that you will always be there
With their head sunk into the pillow and your feet covered with your ruffled duvet sheets
You sit there and watch them sleep
As they do you
And when all words have disappeared until your lips don't speak
You're speechless
You're tired
But you want to tell them a thousand words
That's when you use your language of love
And this is how both persons continue to think, feel, and speak
Because once this non communication is achieved
You then linguistically speak the language of love
And this is the language of your hearts

Rat

I love my sister

It's crazy to think that one day I'll have to wake up without her

I'll make her cups of teas

Make sure she eats

Sometimes it feels like this life is limited between us

But it's okay

Just call me so that I know you got home safe

I want the best for her

My better half

We're like ying and yang

50/50

She'll be the good one

And I'll be the bad one

A balance of characters that was purposely set beyond us

But for us

I'll forever be there for her

That little soft spot I can never get rid of

And even though she calls me crazy

She knows

She knows

She knows there's not a thing I wouldn't do for her

Her will to love me makes me so emotional

And for that...I'm so thankful

Remember when we were thirteen and that girl tried to run up on us

with a knife

And I stood in front of you and said

"Run"

Looking back now

That's when I knew that I'd make sure I get hurt before you do

I never used to......

But as I got older

I realised it was ....

And for that

I'm so grateful

#I love you rat

The Nurture In Love

When you feel lost.... they'll find you
When you're tired.... they'll lay with you
When you need encouragement.... they'll inspire you
When you need a mate...they'll play with you
When you're mad.... they'll listen to you
When you feel deflated.... they'll take their time with you
When you need unity...they'll build this with you
A true love wants the best for you when they are with you
And when they are without you
They will always want to nurture you

Let's....

Let's play like we've got all the energy in the world
Let's lay in bed together and enjoy our ruffled sheets
Let's argue with our entire mite but make up without a fight
Let's hate when we're mad but love harder
Let's trust like no other
Let's hold each other when we cry
Let's laugh and enjoy our fun times
Let's loose ourselves in a tipsy state intoxicated with drink
Let's lay back and watch the world go by when it's busy at its peak
Let's tour the world and view the sun over the beach
Let's talk on the phone until we fall asleep
Let's share our vulnerability and put our hearts on our sleeves
Let's not think with our minds
Let's think with our hearts
And run away with life
Let's create an unbreakable relationship that stays cemented to our committed partnership
There are a lot of things couples should do together such as this
Put it on a posted note
And remember to let the fun in your relationship exist!

Truanted

Absences can make the heart grow fonder
But the heart gets tired of waiting
The heart gets fed up when not acknowledged
Taken for granted
And sometimes... absent becomes the heart

Home

Hold on for them
And they'll will hold on for you
Never let go
And in return they'll will never let go of you
And when you've got nothing left to say
All you can be is do
And with that you will always be there for them
Because you are committed to them
You're loyal and you respect them
Let the presence of your love be a home for them
So, when they need something real
They'll come back to you
And that's how it will always be
Because there are some things we'll never leave

A Superficial Love

Material things can deceive you and make you look attractive
But the heart cannot be clothed
And so, a predictable love is not love at all
An unpredictable love is when real love lets us fall
So, don't be fooled by love at first sight
Because you must fall in love with the being
And not the image you know nothing about

Loves Fire

Throw their love into the surroundings of danger, lies and destruction

And they'll be safe

As long as their holding each other's hands

Their holding on to their trust through the fire

Love Lost in Society

So, lost in my mind
But so, content with my heart
It's a bittersweet parallel
But I feel agitated when both are apart
I look back at a duplicate of my confusion
An unsettled mind I leave for many reasons
It's a bittersweet state of mind
As I can taste my ability to love hard
Which has created a heart dedicated to nurturing another
But I can taste the bitterness of my own rejection
In fear of being perceived as a deluded presence
When faced with those
Who don't understand what I mean....
That the power and act of love is to be appreciated
That equality is essential
And not just in a romantic relationship but for humanity's greater good

I'm looking at the bigger picture of societies paradigm of wealth
And I see degradation within the systematic struggle to attain material assets
Therefore, constructing how individuals in the new age society are valuing their commodities above the basic humans psychological, social, and physiological needs
Synonymously changing the art of how to love and de franchising its value
When it's ultimate unison within the world Is so in need
More so now than ever before

Love lost in society
Love lost in individuals new constructed priorities
Then there was you and me
Attempting to live in our own self-built reality
Whilst your mind knows better than to wear your heart on one's sleeve
in a sinful world
Be a part of society but don't get stuck into society
Don't allow your heart to be poker faced by your mind
As the equilibrium of your love and society can be present in your own
constructed reality

A Sabotaged Love

To all my love less souls

Sometimes you may feel like you may never find true love

Like you're in a whole different head space

And what you're talking about is not being received well

In fear that you may be coming across too strong or way too deep

about things

Though why?

Because society has transformed the way people view love

So, we're soft if we love?

We're desperate if we need?

If language can inhibit a stigma attached to the word 'love'

Then the new age society may be culturally changing others'

perceptions on love

Therefore, losing the art of how to love and the meaning of it

Due to the lack of emphasis of its value not being communicated in

modern society

The sabotage of love it's self

May mean we create a society of individual relations as opposed to

social relations

I can only hope for the world and for the younger generations of our

youth

That love doesn't become a meaningless commodity

And that they do not value their possessions above their social relations

For the harmony of humanity.........I hope

The thing is, from me to you

You're not and nor am I 'deep'

Like minded energies are only touching upon what they know

Surfacing the true understandings of humility, gratitude and well you
can fill this part '   '
But I can't help but feel like my generation has no morals based on the
commitment to others
Do not value love or understand what it means to accept others for
who they are
Or are simply not educated on the practicality of love
2 point 0 said
"Don't mistake my wise words for arrogance"
21 backpacks said ...
"I seeked upon the depths of love and left my generation behind me"
Holding up reversed peace signs as I exit this crowed

Generally, a woman will always seek to love
As most feel content with giving commitment to one spouse
It's such a shame that most males aren't reared to strive for these
same outerisims
I guess even in love...patriarchy still wins
So now were stuck with a head full of thoughts
A heart full of love
With a high chance that due to the complexities of society and peoples
unknowing of self
That you may meet a person who may accept you
But doesn't truly know how to love you

Dedicated to the Love Anthem Outro

I tell them

"Let LOVE Win"

Love is peace

And peace is love

To love is to be humble

To love is to give

To love is to be strong

To love is to care for others

To love is to forgive

Pay honour to the mantra of 'one love' within the genre of reggae and its musical expression for unity

Give me a moment to gather my words and allow me to explain the above

Zarra's definition of love: The selfless being and act to expand oneself for the commitment and wellbeing for others

Love is peace

And peace is love

Look at love now look you

Love will humble you

It is humility which dictates love

Do you attain the virtue of humility within you?

It is humility which will enable you to love genuinely

It is humility which will allow you to adopt the attribute of gratitude

And gratitude will enable you to understand the full discourse of love, forgiveness, and happiness

These attributes are intensely needed in order to circle positive energies around you

But not just for the sake of self
But so that this positive energy can transcend on to others
Watch how the universe generates when love is present
Because love is an energy
Watch how this energy can manoeuvre positivity around you
And those of whom surrender to the love of the higher being
Are the ones of whom will move forward with you
Leave the others and wish them well

Allow me to continue
There's no hierarchy in love
Only the cohesion of love and equality
Your charity for others will enable you to love selflessly
But external ramifications and poor experiences felt may oppose you
And so, love will also challenge you
Your 'strength' and your 'will' to love will be in question
As it is your personal discourse for peace of which is actually challenging you
Therefore, no longer is it love challenging you
But its peace asking you, how much do you need me?
Q. Can you be accountable for your actions, shun your pride and expose your faults to others
Q: Can you seek for peace even when your love is inexistent?
And with those questions present....
Here comes that moment to which your strength and more importantly your will to love will now be tested
Now exposing the true vibrations of your heart and who you are
Pause
To love is to find that little bit of effort for another

Even when were empty and have nothing left to give others
Love will drain you

Can you keep the power of love alive?
But let love not to fool us
To give this type of love to those of whom yet to understand the full
diaspora of love can be tough
As their lack of understanding can distort love

With all the above said
Let me finish
Look at the spirituality of love
Now look you
How much can you kill them with love?
So that you can birth peace
Even when others have forsaken you
Because true love
Is to give love
Even when we are resistant

Chapter 4
Journey 08

'Our own self-identity is a revolutionary of development'
(Z,Hitsburg)

Introduction

S elf-reflection, acceptance, honesty, humility, gratitude, accountability, and positivity plus many other attributes will begin to create one's ontological development of growth. Yes, it can be contended that people never actually or personally change as their character has been settled in assistance of whom they already are. However, 'growth' can enable a person's will to do better to which I highlight that the attributes of 'understanding' and 'acceptance' are the enablers of inner growth.

The anthropology of a human life span enables a person to grow physically from infant to child, adolescence into adulthood and then into elderly age and whilst this manifestation of physical development continues to take place, the inhabitation of our own life experiences also grows in what I call the 'anthropology of the mind'. In sociological terms this is what I would call a 'metaphysical' growth, in which enables the mind to grow mentally, cognitively, and consciously but also sub consciously; whilst being intwined with 'self'. All of which conclusively shapes how we see ourselves, how we see others, how we live with ourselves and how we live with others.

This chapter heavily focuses upon the understandings of the human ontological and metaphysical growth whilst applying applied ethics, normative, metaphysics, etymology and linguistics, as a blueprint to explaining the growth behind the philosophies between right and wrong, virtue and vice, good and evil, mind and matter, potentiality and actuality, change and growth and the necessity of communication. This brings me on to question but state: Is the expectation of the word 'change' just a heavy misconception to the real labelling of the word 'growth', which is really the expansion of development in all dynamics where evolution exists.

My theory behind Journey 08 studies in further detail the development of inner growth. Therefore, this chapter explores the differences between the philosophies between biological development and personal growth, change and leadership, parent and teacher, societal growth and ontological growth. To continue, this chapter continues to explore how honesty and self-reflection plus more is integral to a person understanding themselves but also how this epiphany can lead to self-actualisation. Journey 08 stresses intensely the importance of why parents and teachers must help to support their child's inner ontological growth whilst continuing to mentor/explain how the following attributes such as acceptance, self-love, accountability, responsibility, honesty and being coherent, can all help to lead a person/child to grow with understanding and discussing how gained understanding can produces a settled disposition for thy self's inner core. All of which may help to break parental sins or generational trauma that may be present for some. Additionally, this chapter continues to analyse how self-acceptance can increase a person's level of humility, strength and integrity to be brave and tenacious in the face of obstacles whilst increasing a person ability to love themself and others with bold transparency. Lastly this chapter investigates how the acceptance of oneself, and others can enable people to love others with confidence,

142

transparency, and authenticity.

This chapter concludes by explaining the disparities but assimilation between societal evolution and ontological growth and why, but also how a person must see the beauty in the hidden places around them in order to create and/or sustain a positive thinking character. In conclusion, all attributes discussed throughout this chapter explains how each of these qualities can help to generate a person to create harmony within a person's inner self thus enabling a person to be settled within their own disposition, environment, household, and world.

Biological Development VS Personal Development

We must make a deliberate effort to lose feeling victimized, emotional, ignorant and the home teachings that we have been taught (within reason), in trade to seeking the true ability of 'understanding' thus giving a person the capability to understand themselves, others and situations at hand in order to move forward positively but also with teamwork.

Most believe or hope that biological development throughout adolescence into adulthood will enable a person to become a full curriculum of a decent human bean of whom will grow to uphold and demonstrate good principles and values once fully grown, when aided by good parenting. In hope of the child growing into an adult of whom obtains, good morals, good values, confidence, resilience, honesty, accountability, and responsibility, with a normalised view that with age brings wisdom. With some believing that adults can deal with conflict amicably due to their physical growth (and personal experiences) into adult age. This maybe apparent for some people but is not always the case for most. We all know this could not be further from the truth.

To explain, people in general place a lot of responsibility on the biology of physical development to single handily create/develop a person's maturity and character as part of a person's growth, in hope that once grown they will obtain such qualities including mental and emotional intelligence, responsibility, honesty and accountability as mentioned above once aided with 'good parenting'. You may have heard people say something like "your older now, you should know how to do better". However, what's growth without mentorship? However the qualities needed to validate saying such as these do not necessarily come with general growth and in actual fact sometimes (or most of the time) these attributes needed must be taught through mentorships and examples, given to a child through to their adolescence stage and into their young adult stage and on to their older adult years .....as we never stop learning.

Once this type of mentorship is given it, therefore, shapes a person's character, morality and boundaries and not to mention one's morale's and values. This kind of mentorship will aid a person's cognitive development once guided into understanding right from wrong and understanding how to take responsibility for their own actions and to be fine when being critiqued by others when at fault without feeling belittled. Additionally, mentorship given throughout a person upbringing can also help a person to understand where they position themselves as a person between the disparities of right and wrong, pride and understanding, and how they live with self and others etc. The biology of human development, a person's experiences and general parenting alone cannot enable this type of growth. Self-reflection is something that needs to be prompted and exampled through mentorship to help surface a person's understanding of 'self'.

144

Change VS Growth

Anything regarding change takes time. Change does not take place just because a person grows into an adult or into their later stages of life as explained before and nor does change happen just because one gained wisdom. For change to take place a person must firstly be receptive to change and even more so be open to accepting themself by wanting to be accountable for their own actions. However, most of all a person must be willing to act upon their change. What's the worth of change being recognized without the person acting upon it? at that point it just becomes ignorance when the person is not able to act upon their change for the sake of self and others? This type of recognition just becomes a vacant lesson learnt and ultimately peace will never be birthed as the persons vibrations within their self - acceptance is yet to triumph over their pride. We must remove ourselves from within ourselves in order to truly grasp understanding in all forms.

Change maybe be the biggest misconception to the true development of growth. Growth takes time. Though, even more detriment, is that growth needs 'acceptance' and acceptance was never easy. Because acceptance takes allot of facing one's failures, mishaps and even harder...faults. Once a person is faced with their own fault's this may lead a person to reflect upon their actions and possibly even who they are, to which this may make a person feel low. However, the revolution of growth which can come out of this is tremendous though, only if the learning gained is acted upon 'positively'. Moreover, and more importantly accepting one's faults can lead a person into the trajectory to their own humanisation. Once self-acceptance is present it can enable a person to not be defined by past actions but to be a person of whom takes accountability and possibly gives honesty to all mistakes made. All of which leads the individual to grow cognitively and enables a person to re write what their truth is going to be moving forward in life and how they believe they can do better. As a result, this may give a person the true confidence to be accountable for their positives, negatives and loving who they are through-out all of this. Because clarity and acceptance will have been achieved here. Resulting in the person to not feel threatened upon what others think of them or how they are seen by others because their own self-acceptance will inhibit them to accept themselves in their full discourse. All of which will help to eradicate a person's ignorance or superiority as this person will be able to accept the good and the bad to all things and always see the bigger perspective to all things mentioned.

If one constantly receives information's from a place of superiority or lack of accountability, then this will create a person to become ignorant to the truth thus shaping a person to feel victimised or an easily offended character. Communicating with individuals such as these may become difficult. When people do not enable their growth to surface then as a result, when receiving new knowledge, understandings or opposing views from others it may never be fully received amicably, because the smallest things that people say or do will always threaten their pride and/or confidence.

Moving forward, when acceptance is present it may unlock a person's mind to pay attention to the comprehension of 'understandings' therefore enabling a person to seek for understanding and not feeling convicted when others speak upon topics that they may not fully be informed upon. Therefore, they may not feel belittled when coming across a person of who knows more about something than they do but instead their new ability to seek for understanding may enable them to enjoy listening and learning from others. Because eventually, they may begin to not feel inferior to others of who whole new information but instead they may begin to appreciate the minds and talents from others.

In summary, in order to truly educate oneself in all dimensions of digested knowledge then self-acceptance must be present to which this will help to create a character who seeks to understand the things they yet to discover. As a result, this may enable a person's self-identity to become a revolutionary of continuous powerful development.

However, we all know this is extremely far and few in between as dictatorship might make some people to unfortunately feel valued and heard when input into a position of authority. Because being listened to may have been something that had failed to be given to some individuals throughout their childhood, teenage adolescent and/or early adulthood. As a result, this lack of validation and failure to be listened to can shape individuals to begin to self-validate themselves but this can also be done in a negative manner (if not thought upon positively). For example, one may begin to attempt to enter into competition with others when spoken to due to possibly feeling inferior of knowing less than their counterpart/s, which subsequently results in a person growing with inferiority of feeling wrong. Conversations such as these are a subconscious reminder of their lack of validation and ears when once young thus resulting in a people such as this to feel convicted when faced with those who may know more than them on certain topics.

However, the irony to this, is we all have various talents, we all are great at something, we are not meant to know everything and the only way to learn is not to speak but to listen.

The art of conversations is not to be right or wrong, or to feel convicted when the truth speaks and nor are conversation to be a platform for one to impose their views, annoyance, judgment, dictatorship, and lack of validation onto others, it's okay to be wrong as through our wrongs is when we learn. There is always more than one way of doing things and not just one way; as the art of conversation is to exchange views, opinions, and experiences in hope to create a better understanding of shared knowledge.

Leadership Vs Influence

This leads me on to explain that if change was ever to be grasped upon then it must start with self. At no point will change take place in a household, institution, or any workplace environment if it does not firstly start with those who are in the position of leadership but then secondly using their position to influence others. The acquisition of leadership can be given to people by a tittle and or through status quo but to 'influence' individuals is another practicality to which the praxis of leading by example must be present in order to influence people.

If change is positively acted upon then its outcome of 'influence' is what enables true leadership to impact others. Therefore, if a parent, manager, or CEO wants change within their environment or home then it must start with those in the position of influence (at the top). Once change starts at the top it enables people to see and respect those of whom lead by example thus in hope of their actions filtering down on to others in hope that they will follow in their leaders' footsteps. Therefore, leadership can be a beautiful disposition of change. As the energy within leadership can impact others to do better once being shown how to do it, resulting in a positivity energy to transcend onto others.

Leadership was never easy for these very reasons, and you can only hope that those in position of leadership have found true solace and

148

acceptance within themselves firstly if they wish to lead others. At no point will change in any environment or home be found if accountability, and self-acceptance has not been found from the leader first. As never mind understanding, leadership will be a mere dust in the wind if exampling diligence and self-acceptance are not acted upon within self-first.

The dictatorship within leadership is hardly respected if a person uses their authority to bully or boss others around without illustrating examples of respect for others. At no point is democracy a favourable agency of leadership without the person on the receiving end having an input towards the situation at hand in order to illustrate teamwork. Also, if a person fails to see their leader lead by example first this will cause disharmony as the person's act of leadership will be merely a person who is in charge but does not lead. If a parent wants a home of love, then he or she must show love, if they want a home of honesty then they must illustrate honesty, if parent wants a home of accountability, then they must say sorry and illustrate how it looks to forgive. Not to mention if a CEO wants a work firm of diligence, then he/she must illustrate their own work ethic in return of respect and conformity when expecting others to work hard for him/her. Once achieved this will or should enable the synergy of respect to become full circle with those they are leading as their position of leadership will have an element of respect present for all people thus influencing others to listen to him/her when he or she gives direction or instructions.

Parent & Teacher
Adults, parents, and society in general teach our young people to be resilient, to stand up for themselves and to fight back when under attack

however did they ever remember to teach young people how to love? We wonder why a lot of relationships fail to progress or couples continue to break up but if we do not teach our children how to love themselves then how will they ever understand how to love another? Most people in general may believe that a child grows up due to human development and that life in general and their experiences will teach them to understand what it means to love another person, due to a single feeling felt in hope that this 'feeling' of love will lead them to do right by loved ones or knowing how to forgive and continue to love through challenges. However, this clearly is not the case let alone knowing how to love others. The 'feeling' of love itself does not always lead individuals to do the right thing to say the lease. The readings explained in the chapter of Dedicated to the Love Anthem regarding love, reflection, accountability, harmony, and honesty must be exampled and taught by parents or carer in order to aid a child's or person's growth towards their personal morals, love, self-love, and self-reflection. To state: these are attributes are of which need to be exampled, taught, guided, and given the assistance of self-reflection to young ones thus to ultimately help aid humility, love, understanding, gratitude, and overall acceptance of self and others. However, if a parent is yet to discover their own core of understanding and self-acceptance then the synergy of understanding will be near impossible to teach or transfer to their child.

To conclude, if all the entire teachings are not exampled or taught to children, then this is possibly another reason as to why children will continue to live with the sins of their parents and generational trauma will continue. Of which enables vicious cycles to continue to regulate if not challenged with understanding, dialogue, honesty, and acceptance in order to break the cycles of which was placed before them.

150

What we do know is that poor decisions, lack of opportunity's, poverty, physical violence, neglect, bullying, oppressions, exploitation, and other various forms of abuse plus much more obscurity's that I have not mentioned can all impact upon a person's moral integrity and most of all their humanisation of personal growth. Therefore, where human development may have continued to take place naturally, physically, and transparently throughout our experiences, personal growth on the other hand can easily become a vacant development, yet to be fulfilled and easily damaged when multiple experiences of both negative and abuse plus other traumas occur. Therefore, impacting upon a person's emotional intelligence and understandings. And so, what we're discussing here is the dismantlement of 'inner growth' due to external experiences felt.

Subsequently inner growth unlike human physical development may need assistance (some naturally attain a personal interest of self-growth) to focus on the understandings of self. True wisdom and growth are not something which grows with physicality, it is not something which is handed to people within maturity either and therefore age is only an attributing factor and not the whole factor to the development of a person's growth. A person's inner self does not speak via age but by wisdom therefore age cannot dictate a person's conceptualisation of inner growth. Only an ontological mental growth can enable the growth of a being. What is being explained here is ones 'Ontology' of growth.

As we become more accepting of ourselves; with acceptance becoming the enabler of which gives us control of all aspects within our lives. For example, the entity of self-acceptance can help to contribute towards one's wellbeing, strength, worth and clarity all of which will subsequently enable a person to take control of what one will and will not tolerate, who they are and what they are. Therefore, self-acceptance may possibly lead individuals to gain the strength to nurture their own personal well-being leading to the establishment of self-love. This is not to say that the support and love from others is not just as important because it is.

However as mentioned, that one's inner growth must be assisted delicately from a child and into adolescence and beyond thus delivered by a parent or mentor via avid communication for the child to then act upon their own principles and morals pragmatically, once reaching into adulthood. All of which can only help to create a person of whom critically questions self, with a focus to understand, progress and become a more positively full rounded improved version of themselves. It all bores down to self.

To continue, a parent must do their child a favour by living honestly within their own truth first and give their child the tools needed to create their own inner growth (when the time is right). In hope of rearing their child to be a person of whom self reflects, reconciles, attains inner strength, obtains humility and gratitude, understands themselves but also understands the power of love and is confident within their own being, with a hope to always do better. However, this must be exampled first, this must be exampled by both parents or parents because parent/s will always be the child's first example of how and why to do better when faced with obstacles in life. At no point will change within a person's home, in children and in families ever take place if it has not taken place within the parent themselves first. Because ultimately parents are the leaders, influencers and always the first teacher the child will learn from. If a child is to do better when faced with conflict, disagreements, battles, and faults then not only will the teacher need to verbally teach the child upon why they must do better, but the child must also be shown 'how' to do better thus by being demonstrated by viewing their parent's actions and illustrations first. Therefore, words always work in conjunction with actions as the combination of both words and action can helps to create justice, love, protection, protests and respect plus more once a person's words and actions are in sync with each other thus enabling language to bring words into action. Words are powerful and without words one would not be able to act, listen, learn or do.

Parenthood Vs Childhood

However, regarding our parents it is important to remember that they are tyring there hardest to parent their child/children to their best abilities and are not always to be blamed as all they have is their own childhood and overall life experiences in life to draw from. Not all persons may be able to be critical thinkers or are able think outside of the box and so they consciously and subconsciously pass on both the good and the bad of what they themselves have been taught. Because they may not always be able to be objective upon the things that they themselves have been taught within their youth and simply because no person is perfect. Though, if an effort of self-improvement is present then the above stated may help to give children a revamped form of parenting and learnings that their own children may need in order to be nurtured within an ever-changing world.

Times change, the world and the environment within nature will continue to manifest both societally and globally thus dictating how people socialise, teach and parent in general. Therefore, as society continues to circulate it is important that parents attempt to practice a new way of thinking and therefore a new way of parenting as their child/children are growing up in an era of which they did not develop or grow in. At no point must people forget tradition as the mixture of tradition and modernity both has its positives and so this must be held on to as both tradition and modernity must be attempted to be given to children as a balance within parenting, in order to create a new practicality of parenting in the new aged society. Both tradition and modernity in parenting cannot be present without one model causing a conflict of interest; if a person leans to one side too much. Possibly resulting in the child to feel emotionally upset and unable to speak thus impacting the child's ability to give respect to their parent/parents of which the parent demands (if the parenting given is too rigid). As a result If reasoning is not achieved, then the parent/s may be left feeling frustrated or confused upon how to parent their children. Moreover, if the parent themselves does not know how to be more flexible within their parenting skills, are too stagnant upon their own ideas, or if they stick to what they know each time, parent out of fear, overly lean on tradition, or are not open to learning a new way of viewing things when parenting their own children, then a distance may take place. As a result, all the above could possibly lead the parent/s to feel even more frustrated each time they are not respected when they give orders to their children and the child continuously resists.

This duality could lead some parents failing to create a united relationship with their children causing the foundations of mutual respect and open understanding (and any other attribute that the parent wishes to build) to be sabotaged thus causing a distance between the parent and child. As in all relationships irrespective of parenting, if any persons are afraid to communicate with the other person, then the relationship will always be fragile.

Each child needs to be nurtured in a different way from their siblings because each child's character and emotions is unique to them. Each child is seeing and interpreting things differently from their siblings and not to mention that they are experiencing different things in their own lives therefore causing each child's personal needs to differ from their siblings. And so, each child may need to be given a different given type of nurturing in comparison to their siblings because each child's character, wants, insecurities, resilience, confidence, and way of thinking is different, therefore meaning each child's 'core needs' are different. Moreover, if open communication, listening, honesty, respect, and understanding is not given or nurtured throughout childhood, adolescent, and adulthood then this could also lead parents to only understand their child to a surface level. If this closeness is not present then parents may become excluded and not know their child's 'full' vibrations such as the child's thoughts, views, feelings, values, morale's etc and overall, who they truly are.

Children will come and challenge their parents; children will come and grow their parents because we never stop learning and sometimes children are a part of a parent's own development and growth. If people continue to learn throughout life, then this same mantra should apply to parenting as children will come along seeing new things that we yet to discover due to the new revolutionised world that they are growing up in i.e., social media and so forth. And so, children themselves enable parents to learn a new way of thinking just by just being around them. The innocence in children is one to be protected but also enjoyed because children are fun, their innocents, their minds and their lack of fear is to be shared and this why parenting is a pleasure. This type of shared space Is a great reciprocation of learning between young and old and parent and child. Though it is important to remember that there is only so much that parents can do, and parents cannot control their child over the worlds influence, that's impossible. Subsequently, all parents can do is try to educate their child the best way they know how.

When people have children, it can be seen as a selfish decision as the child never asked to be present. However, when a parent enables themselves to grow as a person first and then as a parent secondly, then this is when the selfishness can be expelled. Because once a parent gives the tools which they have used to preserver with throughout life and they then give these same tools back to their child; thus, given through protection and guidance. It is this mentorship where the child receives the fruits to a parent's labour thus giving the child an example to learn from when faced with challenges in life and much more. Just delivered through a parent's guidance, protection, support and always love, making the selfishness obsolete.

Nature Vs Society
As the nature of the world continues to manifest through wars, animal distinction, natural erosion and industrialisation thus changing the nature of the world and with people creating a revolutionised society, this conclusively enforces people in society to live in an ever-changing environment in comparison to previous centuries. As a result of this societal change, individuals in the new aged century have now become accustomed to living in and under new multiple agencies of connections thus delivered through over saturated propaganda, mis education and social media and so forth. Then the element of 'nurture' in parallel to nature may also continue to also change. The basic element of 'how we nurture others' may have also changed due to the development of

society's newfound connections and information. Thus, changing the way people reach out to contact others. As our level of communication with people has now become broader i.e., apps, emails, etc therefore enabling people's delivery of showing compassion for people to also be broader but also much more intricate than previous centuries. As digital technologies have revolutionised the way society communicates and has therefore become a normality within society, it also simultaneously gives people in society multiple complexities to the things that they are exposed to and the things that they learn from. Overall changing the way people in society communicate with each other and changing the way they show compassion and care to others. To explain, wishing a person happy birthday was once strictly given only via a card or in some cases a fax machine however due to the development of digital technology we now have smart phones and emails etc all of which allows individuals to use different technological outlets to illustrate their care and acknowledgment of others and so it can be argued that technology is changing the way that that people in the 21st century show care.

Therefore, if the element of 'nurturing others' in parallel to societies evolution continues to evolve between technology and society; then these mechanisms may have changed the frameworks of how people communicate with others due to the expanding multiple agencies of technology. All of which may have not only changed the way people communicate with others, but it may have also transformed the way in which people in the new aged society nurture others of whom they care for. Therefore, due to social media I question: has the compassion in nurturing others become less intense than before or more intense than ever?

Children in the 21st century are now growing though the eras of technology (exposing them to the access of more information than their parents and possibly putting them under more pressure to blend in). Therefore, as mentioned before it is clear that parents must also move with society's developments and therefore change the way in which they parent (within reason) whilst keeping the balance of tradition and modernity present and holding onto great dialogue within communication with their child/children in order avoid the miss information that social media can cause. It may be important for parents to be aware of the impact of social media and attempt to avoid social media from becoming the primary agency which teaches their offspring. Therefore, it could be suggested that parents within the 21st century have a lot more responsibility to intentionally teach their children good values than in comparison to previous generations due to the rise of social media and not to mention an ever-changing UK education curriculum. In conclusion a balance between teaching and communication must be consistently kept enabling parents to be the primary teachers to their children and to keep the understandings and bond between parent and child present. With a hope of keeping the principles of love present when communicating with their offspring in order to keep the foundations of love present within their children's development.

Good Parenting Vs Honest Parenting

I stress that no person or parent is perfect and nor is there a book to draw from regarding how to parent another human being, no person walking is perfect and so fault will happen which is evitable. However, a parent of whom speaks to their children with open honesty about their own faults made whilst parenting them is all a child can ask for and they must listen to their elders. However, it is also important for the child to respect and appreciate their parent's efforts as ultimately, we would like to believe that parents have tried their best. Because at some point children will grow up and they will begin to question the decisions made by their parents and it is important that parents give their children their own truths in order for their offspring to grow with ease, understanding and clarity thus enabling the child to move forward into an adult of who is living within their own identity, clarity and walking in their own truth. As mentioned, parents are only human too and they can only try and through trying people make mistakes. If a parent's love for their offspring overrides everything within them as a person, then the humility and gratitude within their own vibrations of love should disregard their own ignorance and pride, in trade of keeping peace close. The exchange of giving honesty to a child can possibly build respect and unity between parent and child. However, if honesty is not given to the child/children, then this may cause a distance and lack of understanding between the parent and child.

To conclude, nothing and no one is perfect, and no one can be taught to be perfect and so blame is not to be placed. People can only help to assist children towards their own personal growth and parents can only give them the tools to do so. And not oppress them or complain about their children being difficult or complain about their children's constant questioning as the innocence in children is which leads them to want to know more and so it is imperative that parents continue to teach. However, adversely a parent can do there upmost to do right by their children and teach them the right from wrong, lead by example, nurture, protect and support them and give them truths and anything else that the child may need however somethings are out of the parents control and so none the less the rest is down to the child.

Societal Evolution Vs Ontological Growth

An ontological growth enables a person's being, existence and reality to be vastly grouped together and once recognised it will aid a person to step into their growth as a circled 'being'. However, with so many distractions in the world people can easily become a product of their environment which holds both positives but also negatives if one's environment shapes who they are. This causes limitations to individuals' ability to understand and critique, as its always beneficiary to think outside the box. What I am explaining here is that the expectations and pressures of the world can sabotage an individual's ontological growth.

To explain, the discourses of people's reality has been structured around ideologies and conditioning which is advocated through society's stratifications within marginalisation's, oppression, systems, injustice's, inequalities, constructs, and categorizations etc all of which will create a confusion upon what is reality and what is deception both internally and externally within a person's being. Subsequently impacting upon people's values, morality and how people socialize and how they see themselves and others. To continue, the more society manifests throughout the centuries is the more some people become more in sync with a scripted globalised culture of a constructed reality which is given to individuals through various influences such as the media and propaganda information and imagery thus delivered through celebrities and sports stars trends, education curriculum, education syllabus and politicians democracy's and so forth. All of which will subsequently birth a fake actuality of reality therefore causing a deception within how people see reality and more so impacting, deducting, or influencing individual's personal values, morale's, and priorities.

This blinded mental conformism is also dictated to people in society through various areas of cognitive processes and socialisms such as the

160

fear of financial instability and traditional and societal expectations. All governed through platforms of power within global authority, political and social hierarchy, and governmental dictatorship. Overall influencing and impacting upon how people are seen symbolically (i.e., race, sexuality, and gender etc) and how people view other. Ultimately taking away people's true ability to think outside the box and be there true authentic self and instead somewhat becoming brainwashed as a result.

Hierarchy and systematic power will synonymously govern people to conform to the positions of hierarchal order and supreme masses will continue to use the entity of cognitive financial fear to advocate this. With this said, once a person does not wish to conform to societal or social order, they may be at risk of being seen as not 'normal' an 'outcast' or 'difficult'. When ultimately true equality would avoid a person from being placed above or below anyone and would ethically avoid a person to be summoned to perform a pre dispositioned role that was given to them by someone else's.

If people are left to conform to society's values and dictatorship then this type of social order removes a person's ability to critique, question and understand oneself and others, their growth and environment. Some individuals may view knowledge and understanding as 'deep' in which one can contend here that people and our new generations possible lack of substance (for some but not all) may enforce them to view things as deep when viewing anything beyond their daily environment, beyond society's construction of normality and beyond their own understandings. This can be debated as a clear example of what happens when society takes away people's ability to question and critique the things they do not understand. Causing a lack of ontological inner growth for some individuals in the new aged society. In conclusion, society at large will take away one's inner ontological growth and humility if people continue to pay attention to societal influences, and expectations, instead of creating their own reality and harmony.

Self-reflection and understanding oneself, as stressed before must be either taught, assisted, exampled or guided, (or possibly all four) throughout a person's development as there are too many distractions of the world that will sabotage a person's ability to understand themselves and others and much more. In addition, there are many injustices, inequalities, divisions, and lack of unity that can easily impact the way people learn and the way people respect others. In contrary, these factors I've explained within the influence of global power and systematic constructs of conformity will increase the miss education within civilisation and cause overall ignorance.

However, I must state that people can become more of themselves in relation to the worlds misery but only if they seek to see the positives globally to everything around them. This will advocate a positive outlook and mindset within themselves and within their environment; whilst living in and through the world's destructions. For this synergy to surface, one must see the beauty in hidden places around them. For example one must seek to see the beauty in the acts of kindness that doesn't always get enough media attention and one must see the beauty in the people who are different from them and see the beauty of other races, ethnicities, religions and cultures etc and not be afraid to socially or romantically integrate and or socialise with others of whom are not like them (due to i.e. cultural normatives that in some areas have been created out of superiority, patriarchy, ignorance, prejudice, fear, or laziness). One must seek to see the beauty to the things that do not directly impact them but be happy for others. However, people will only begin to see beauty in hidden places once taking a step back to view. People must not limit themselves to what they already know or by the

162

things that they see, or only care for the things which only related to themselves.

We never get old from learning new things and whilst the world continues to manifest; if one thinks positively, is honest, attains acceptance for others, upholds accountability and responsibility for their actions (decisions making, rights and wrong), attempts to understand, attains humility and gratitude, accepts positive criticism, does not feel belittled when at fault and loves self then one will be led towards their own self-actualization. With self-actualisation discovered it will form the true discovery of self. Where one will begin to learn from themselves and open to learning from others. Overall enabling one to become more of themselves and embody the true essence of who they are and who they have become. It is important to stress that no person is perfect or has all the attributes that I have explained throughout this chapter or entire book. People make mistakes and struggle at times however a real one told me that were only human and that's okay and with that said all people can do is put love first, be honest, be responsible and accountable and always try to do better.

Journey 08 the poetic literature explores the true development of self-growth via entwined words of which speak to a person's inner self. Journey 08 the literature has a heavy focus upon self-reflection of which converses inside the philosophies between wrong and right, obstacles within life and the full diaspora between truth, trust, honesty, loyalty, empathy, justice, teamwork, respect, accountability, love, peace and more; whilst highlighting how individuals are the generators of positive change both internally, externally, socially, and globally.

Journey 08
The Poetry

Welcome to Journey 08

Looking down at the world

Below a glowing sea

Mediterranean breeze

Glowing sun rays shine upon each engines wing

Distorted clouds

Altitude under one's feet

So many more steps to take

Intrigued

Rejuvenating

Letting destiny take its place

Learning to accept the things that are beyond one's control

80th's very own

0.8 to right now

Positive minds

Truth over fake

Journey 08

08's Very Own

I'm sure you've heard it before
"One must love themselves in order to love somebody else"
A broken record of words
With multiple replays
Lost its criticality
Without a melody to decipher its personal intake
With youthful minds one will critique what they expect from a spouse
However, a person entwined with 'self' will critique what they expect from themselves
Taking full accountability for their good, there bad, their actions, their behaviour, their rights, and their wrongs
Thus, promoting the fluidity of critical thinking
Leading one to question their qualities, there morals, there values, there justice, their passions, there worth, their strengths and their weakness's
Resulting In an overall cylinder of self-reflection
Therefore, learning the true understandings of who they are
Only time, self-reflection, acceptance, honesty, and experiences can advocate this

Did you look at your own qualities with a deep sense of self-worth and appreciation?
Did you attempt to self-reflect and lose your ignorance for the trade of self-actualisation?
Thus, birthing a true sense of self discovery
Loving the trajectory of your growth
Acquiring ownership to who you are transparently
Ultimately loving who you are personally

However, let life not fool us
'Change' is a part of the process
People change
Human beings are a development of the manifestation upon change
Our experiences, our environment, our adventures, and our desires will
have all had its impact within our lives
Changing the way, we view things
However, some stay true to their foundations
Understanding the disparities between the things that they want from
the things that they need
And remaining true to their principles regardless of the situations

Now ask yourself
Is love a requirement you believe life just brings?
Or is love an attachment of a deep intimacy that you need?
Life may mentally and emotionally move you
However, when you have clarity upon who you are
When you have a deep sense of self worth
When you know what you need
And when you know what you have to offer
You will seek for a partner who will appreciate what you have to bring
As it is only the learning's from self-love
That can teach you how to give love

19

The state of mind is a powerful thing

One shall use their mind and not just think

Mind the media

Subliminal messages jump out of the screen

Be unique one should love thee

Though one shall do on to others as they do on to themselves

Weigh nobody lesser or above regardless be a part of a team

As equal people we shall not fear one another

But only fear god

With only our eyes to view

We should never judge

Money is regulated

Greed is a sin

Nothing can compare with the happiness from within

Be a part of society but do not get stuck in society

Remember the finer the things

A shallow and narrow mind is what keeps insecurities mainstream

Do you make sense of it all?

Always see the bigger picture

Happiness, health and good wellbeing is hard yet easy to come by

Some things go wrong

What can make it right?

A powerful thing is the state of mind

2 point 0

"Don't mistake my wise words for arrogance"

21 Backpacks

I journeyed towards the depths of love and left my generation behind

me

Ontological 22

Our own self-identity is a revolutionary of development
Just like society that continues to manifest in parallel with this
So, we continue to be more ourselves, learning, growing and being
Basing our own self change on whatever our morals and values are
These are the things that we live by, that shape us and make us more
entwined with ourselves and influence how we live with ourselves and
within our social relations with others
Ultimately humanising who we are

The 22nd Whisper

When ignorance takes over
A lack of understanding could never challenge what it does not know
Because those who think they are right all the time
Or listen to respond as opposed to understand
Do not allow their knowledge or self to grow
And so, they limit themselves to what everybody else already knows
Those who believe themselves to be right all of the time
Are so right that they may be so unaware of how wrong they actually
are

However, this behaviour is only an illustration of how much they feel
belittled when spoken to
This may also be an illustration of how much someone previously failed
to listen to them and/or validate them
Until this lack of validation transformed into one's ignorance
As a result, communication and/or reasoning became obsolete
As their ears no longer listen when new understandings speak
A wise person will have more questions than answers
But a wise person will use their ears to understand
One must listen and learn from others
As only a fool doesn't want to be corrected

22 Building Blocks

If a man says he does not love loose women
But continues to have sexual encounters with them
Then he just gave that 'loose female' one of the best parts of himself
'His body'
So, in actual fact it is not the women that he does not love
But himself
Self-affiliated by his association with his female counter parts
Who are reflections of his own self-value
Do not be a male who loves multiple women forever
Experience the love of commitment and loyalty
And for your spouse, you loved another's soul
And you will be a man who built a home

23 Leaders

Strong characters love to be in charge
But a balanced character is diplomatic
And knows when to lead

Shelf 23 Book 30

When the injustice is immense

And sadness, revenge, unfortunate events allure its transparency

It is only normal to question .... why?

As certain events can consume us

And infiltrates our thinking, thought process and understandings

Anxiety can take place

Confusion sets in

However

Stop asking 'why'?

As It's best to just live life and maybe you'll discover the answers along the way

Or maybe you won't and that's okay

As if the answers do not reveal itself

The teachings always will

As if you trust in faith and positivity

You may learn how to believe in the things that you cannot see

As you may then learn how to trust; that all things can be for the greater good

All put in place to better ....you

But only if accept accountability and seek understanding

Thus, leading to personal growth

But only If you choose to see the positives to all negative situations

But only if you trustingly 'act upon' your positives learnt to better 'yourself'

This will lead you to see the positives from all poor experiences that you've endured

Growth: Cannot and will not take place if one fails to see or admit fault

And nor will growth take place if a person does not put into practice what they have learnt

If not

Cycles will continue to repeat themselves

And, well justice and harmony will be absent within a person's energy

Therefore, justice and harmony will be something that this person will
not know how to give

...............Stuck

If the answers do not reveal itself

The teachings always will

Some independently acquire wisdom through personal growth thus
taught by themselves

Some see their answers of their own truths on their canvas

However, ignorance, wrath, carelessness and/or pride plus more
withholding them from acting upon what they have learnt

Some acquire wisdom through mentorship

But most acquire wisdom due to time and getting older

They see the truths on their canvas

However, their emotions distort their eyes, heart, and mind and so the
lessons stare at them blind

Nevertheless, they are left none the wiser

And so, you find that the answers are in your experiences

And so, you find that the answers are in the teachings

Overall, you find that the answers are in what you have learnt

Stop asking 'why'?

It's best to just live life and maybe you'll discover the answers along the
way

Or maybe you won't and that's okay

Some grow from their lessons, admit fault and acceptance, and move

forward with positive energies
Thus, becoming a more rounded being
Enabling them to be a person who can create an environment of
understating, harmony, peace, love, respect, and equality due to
their.... open honesty
However, some stay stagnant and see a fictional version themselves
Therefore, becoming stuck with dim energies
Thus, withholding their personal growth due to whatever it is they are
battling with

If the answers do not reveal itself
The lessons always will
Lessons instilled within us enables us to deal with challenges and
oppositions
And you'll be given all the tools needed in order to handle but also
battle against all trials and tribulations
'Fight the good fight'
However, it is up to you to act upon what you have learnt
Disregarding pride, fear, arrogance, and ignorance plus more
Done, for the love of inner peace
And for the love of external harmony
Subsequently allowing one's energy to grow with love and acceptance
and without ignorance
Overall: Enable your lessons now learnt to create your own peace and
harmony
However, your lessons learnt will 'mean nothing' if you do not embody
true acceptance upon the situation at hand
With ull the above said
Teachings and lessons will never create perfection
No one was made to walk perfectly

We were made in perfection with great imperfections
Even the wises people make mistakes
Therefore, it is not always the mistakes that we are judged upon
But what we choose to do with our lessons learnt once the event has
past
I State: One's morality and values as a person will be in question, once
learning certain truths but failing to try to correct one's wrongs
'Effort' will always be merited
So, if you were looking for answers
Then seek to learn
But seek to attain the courage and humility to do better
And expose your faults in trade for the love from others
As karma was always around the corner
The universe was never asleep

And so, you find that the answers are in the teachings
And so, you find that the answers are in what you have learnt
And as for your injustices felt, which opposed your will
Be fearless and take hold of your strength with love and with both
hands
We all fall down from time to time
But time will heal
Your disposition will re-occur
Your fight against anger, fear, doubt, or struggles will lead you into
happiness
If you accept fault
And hold on to faith

Head To: Staircase 24 Classroom 30

We teach our children to fight and defend themselves
But we don't teach our children how to love
"I love you" says the young child
"I love you too" says the parent
To know love is not inhibited with 'just a feeling'
This feeling is not merited just because it's a feeling felt
To feel love and to understand love are two different acquisitions
The more a person grows the more the meaning of love becomes
subjective to oneself
The more this aids the development of self-love
As the understandings of love is one that needs to be given patience
Given a moment to be taught
Given a moment to grow
And to be learnt
The power of education can spread love
If you take a moment to teach love
Imagine the possibilities of change

The 24th Observation

If you sit back and watch people for their actions
Sometimes people may shock you
When you grasp upon life experiences, knowledge, and wisdom
You begin to learn the true understandings of love, justice, and unity in
parallel to those around you
It's that moment that you begin to realise that people are not what you
thought they were
And understand that in certain situations; you must know when to have
the courage to speak and when to be silent
But you also begin to learn that sometimes
Its best to accept imperfection
It's best to remember that no person is perfect
It's best to let others do them
Because sometimes it's more powerful to observe
Then it is to use words

Gate 25

You should illustrate your will
Continue to attain love for those who have love for you
But also attain love for those who do not have love for you
If you are unable to communicate through difficult situations
Due to pride, ignorance, fear, or self-righteousness and so forth
Then your relationship with those around you will always be fragile

One must look at the bigger picture
Put things into perspective
Who are you to hate?
Why should you hold malice and disregard for anyone?
*If no one is perfect, then how much can you subscribe to this when
others do you wrong?*
Accept the differences from person to person
Build their strength when they feel weak
Guide them when they feel lost
Show them how to correct their wrongs
Support them when they are feeling low
Educate them to know more
However, one must be open to others correcting thee
And not reject guidance due to feeling belittled when others speak
Ultimately accept others for who they are
But forgive others for what they have done
As I was once told
They do not know what they are doing
Some know better
Some do better
Do better

Remember that your differences are what make our socialisms a
superior experience
'Sorry' a hard word to say, even harder to mean
'Respect' something we should give to one another equally
'Pride' hard to put aside
But sometimes it is the greatest thing we can ever do
In order to accept our faults and come clean
Even better when we hold no grudge and move forward together as a
team

25 Changes

Nothing you wear defines you
Only your heart defines you
No worldly possessions will keep your soul happy
Hard work does not always give you blessings
Pay attention to the things that change your moods
Live right by yourself and others and small blessings will follow you
Be brave in the face of change
However, when you've outgrown your surroundings, and everything is the same
Change is what is needed
As your old routine is no longer the life that excites you anymore
And you find yourself daydreaming about the new plans you wish to embark upon
This is when change needs to be seeked
When the vibrancy around you turned dull and your reds became brown
And your whites became grey
You need to change the colours you wake up to everyday
Or maybe this change isn't a change period within your life
Maybe it is a transition in your life that you need to begin living
As a new challenge is something you stepped forward into and now need
In order to move forward towards the blessings that you must receive
Where you must work hard, show gratitude, and keep believing
That everything happens for a reason

Ticket 26

Life is like a freely scripted drama on stage
And the leading role is you
And you have no idea what the next scene will be or who will be in it
And you can only play the role that you were given
But the dramas continue
Both good and bad actor's play their part
Until one day you become a veteran to the stage
And the theatre becomes a playground of your life's most memorable
moments
And one day you sit back and reminisce on a theatre act
That was the best live show you'd ever seen
As your life on stage was the best part of each scene

26 To Right Now

Time is of the essence

Life comes along and brings its blessings

When time moves so fast

And new endings bring new beginnings

One must soak up the good times

Live fast in the moment

Without abusing it

Or you'll lose it

Live high

And manage the lows

Enjoy the best moments

And grab life with both hands

Enjoy your achievements

And enjoy your mistakes

As it was a great lesson learned

Have no shame in owning your faults

Where would we be if we didn't fail in order to appreciate the times

when our success wins

Be proud of the person you are

Be proud of those around you

Love hard, be happy and laugh

And leave pride behind you

It's funny how time goes by quickly when we're having fun

So, live while you're young and even old

As no one ever dies

We just continue to live on through our souls

26 Ribbons

Almost all males prefer sons and fear having a daughter
Due to the same rehearing that they give to their boy children to
fornicate
It's easy to avoid than it is to self-reflect and to admit fault
As a result, most oppress females and de-value there worth as new-
borns
Thus, penalising women at the hands of men's lustful actions
A son enables one to perpetuate selfish actions
However, a daughter forces one to be a protector from males who are
mirror of themselves
It's easier to seek power than it is to seek humility
Most fail to recognise the paradigm of self-reflection and development
It's easy to raise a son
However, it is harder to raise a son to be a good man
Especially if it is something, they've never been

The 27th Glow

Find it in you to remain calm

Disputes can be handled amicably

No need for arguments

Attempt to be wise in conflict

Perpetuate the value of teamwork

Remind yourself of your success

Listen and learn from others

Remember to put loved ones before thy self

Love to love

Fear only the lord

Be clear upon your statements

Communicate your courage

Critique ignorance

Applaud strength

And continue to learn the depths to understandings that you were once

naive to

To create an armour of un-touch ability

That those in fear cannot challenge

And only external counterparts with authentic minds will see your

strength as peace

When they look at you

27 PM

Before you give up
Maximise all opportunity's
Exhaust all resources
Leave with nothing more to give
And if it doesn't work out
Relax, reflect, and evaluate
And when you're ready.....go again
Patience: Nothing before its time
No such thing as giving up
Everything has its place
Positive energy for those who believe.....
Timing is everything

27 Cylinders

Life can be very cyclical

When similar experiences happen more than once

And this puts your life into perspective for you to learn

And then you attempt to add up your lessons learnt to discover the

answers

Whilst remembering that some things are beyond you

But paying attention to the repetitive circumstances that forces you to

grow

However not everyone grows old

Age may represent multiple variables upon the external being

But growth was never a factor of age

Not everyone's grows old

Though if you accept your faults

And if you accept truths

If you accept self

If you seek for humility

If you embody support, comprehension, and love

Clarity will be in your view

It is at this moment that the crossroads of change will be looking right

at you

Only those who find the strength to submit their change to the

principles and power of love and justice will be at ease

This tranquillity of ease and peace will enable you to reflect and

understand a picture painted of the life you live, love, and now see

The 28th Plan

The universe has its plans in place for you

Live just

Walk with wisdom

Spread love

Effort will always be commendable

Be genuine with your actions

Ask no questions

Something's are beyond you

Accept the things beyond your control

Trust your strength

Share wisdom and positivity

Seek growth

Manifest your personal development

Fear only God

Give thanks

Easier said than done

Deliverance from temptation

Be accountable for your sins

Repent

It's okay to make mistakes

We can all do better

Walk towards the sun and serve God only

Serve the Ten Commandments

Set no expectations, seek no glory, pray, and walk towards your salvation

All of the above is only rationalised adherents of the proverbs we must keep

But it counts for nothing if you don't believe

Your struggle is one that can help you to break the cycles that those
before you of whom failed
Your struggle is one that can help those who are in need
Sometimes you must go through turmoil and destruction to really
acquire the passion to make change
And that's the beauty from the pain

PRIDE 29

There are three things that you cannot achieve with a person who is
ignorant
You cannot influence ignorance
You cannot reason with ignorance
You cannot create teamwork with ignorance
Because a wise soul cannot create peace with PRIDE

The 29th Assimilation

When you 'know' something, someone or was told of a situation
It has an effect on your cognitive thinking
Therefore, giving you the 'know how' upon how to handle a possible
situation or person
However, this can also be counterproductive
As just because you 'know' something
Doesn't mean you know at all
As they may have a scripted morality upon what is best

When you 'feel' something or someone when told of a situation
It moves your consciousness
Enabling you to subconsciously reflect upon the situation at hand,
where your feelings dictate your responses and given understandings
To know and to feel are two great differences of disparities
Between the cognitive and consciousness
A lot of people are knowing
But there not feeling

Do not look for advice from those of whom 'know'
Even if they are polished and well experienced
But seek affirmation, advice, and guidance from those who 'feel'
As those of whom feel over what they know
Respond with assimilation, shared familiarity, and recognition
Those of whom feel situations will not be lost for words upon what you
can try, consider or do
Because they resonate with you through familiarity
And they use this paradigm to understand the feet that walks in your
shoes

The 30th Truth The Whole Truth And Nothing But The … Honesty

It's best to lower your principles upon others morality
It's best to lower your expectations upon people's morals
And accept that the truth upon self; hurts others to admit it more, than it may do you
Furthermore, accept that people are subconsciously in favour of pride and being right
This is when people begin to argue and fight
Sad but true
As only a holy heart can bear fault
As only the very few seek to understand before they defend
Only some people have the spiritual strength to lean towards their love and not pride
Not everyone's energy has true empathy inside
Because....you can't teach heart

The more people in any form of a relationship call out for others to give honesty; in which is not returned
Are the more individuals maybe placing themselves in a position of which enables them to be depicted as an initiator of conflict
As appose to an initiator of honesty
Excepting honesty from a person who is yet to be vulnerable or accept themselves might make you come across......crazy
You can speak societally but true harmony speaks spirituality

The truth brings peace
Peace is love
But love is tough if the heart is not soft

To love is to be humbled but not if it remains tough
It is only normal to defend oneself
But after a dispute most like to defend their thrown even when wrong
You ask why?
Because the truth makes others question their decisions, actions and so
forth
This causes a person to question 'self'
Exposing to themselves their own heart
A red reflection, zooned in and focused upon thee
They may now start to see
That they maybe not be who they thought they were
And now the truth made there being feel low and naked
But a real one will bear no judgment and seek to clothe you

Therefore, to expect the truth from others is to expect that a person has
already reached a place of acceptance within themselves

And maybe it's not necessarily their wrongs that need to be accepted
But maybe it is who they are that needs to be accepted
And maybe they are not there yet
Or maybe they are unaware of self
Or maybe they are aware of self, but cannot accept fault; as never mind
being wrong
The acceptance of who they are............ simply hurts too much

I'm not that bad?
One questions
And it is this missing lack of self-acceptance within a person's thought
processing or being which causes them to defend themselves
Or simply.....ignorance

196

Be positively confident as no person is better than the other
Were all equals

Ignorance is easy
But growth was always hard
And growth may be easy for some... but not for others
And some people may never get there
And that's fine
As everyone is different
Live your truth
And so overall
You may be doing yourself an injustice by calling out for the truth
As it may only backfire upon you
You ask why?
Because we live in a sinful world in which people are not always humble
enough to trade in their pride for humility
And accept themselves for the sake of peace

Therefore, individuals may be doing themselves an injustice
As the more one demands the truth
The more others argue
Which may only adversely enable truth callers to be perceived as a
conflictual individual
Honesty is a virtue
Because honesty births growth
Growth enables teamwork
Teamwork helps others
And what's the opposite of teamwork
'I'

And 'I' can be selfish

And it's a selfish world

So, don't expect peace from a world that inhibits greed...which inhibits

sin

Sin has a great way to make the good look bad

And bad energies seek to keep the good down

Hurt people hurt people

But a bad energy seek to damage

So instead of letting negative energies shape how you are seen

Say nothing

Observe

Know when to speak

When to be silent

And when to have courage

Because ultimately you cannot expect others moral compass to be like

yours

But do not be discouraged by this

And so, remain locked within your own morals, principles, and virtues

Expect no truths from others

And let others damage themselves with their own lies, lack of

accountability and deception

And so you see.....that's why telling the truth is so hard

As its' a reflection upon who a person is

Although they say nobody's perfect

This is easier said than ....no not done

But easier said to others than said to self

People make mistakes

And this is perfectly okay

From our mistakes is when growth can be made
And growth can be a beautiful state of time
Who wants to be right all the time
It's better to grow than it is to be right …..right?
And so, mistakes are okay
As the manifestation of a person's beautiful development comes next if humility is kept close
If pride becomes non-existent within this moment
If an 'independent' sorry is the next words given
To illustrate that……their trying
Then respect and teamwork can now commence
How this is received is down to you

But as mentioned above…. lower your expectations and don't seek for certain responses from others
One must sooth their own needs
Create your own strength, with wisdom and harmony
But continue to wish others well
Just done with distance if necessary
Because
They say the truth will set you free
Or you will fight from within
And a person who cannot accept their faults
Or accept others
May never feel the peace that true humility brings

Acknowledgements

I would like to dedicate this book to my grandmother E.E.B.M for being the person of whom taught and built my strength and resilience as a woman. For recognising my talents, for continuing to guide and direct me and for always giving me encouragement, support, and ears when I needed. Lastly, I would like to say thank you for loving me unconditionally and for always being my example and my role model. I'm forever filled with humility and gratitude to of had her as a grandmother. Words will forever fail me when explaining how special and great she is. She's amazing, she's strong, she's got heart, she leads by example, she's simply exceptional.

I Love You & Thank You.

Zarra Hitsburg

Printed in Great Britain
by Amazon